CAMBRIDGE UNIVERSITY PRESS

CAMBRIDGE ENGLISH Language Assessment
Part of the University of Cambridge

Cambridge English

PROFICIENCY

CERTIFICATE OF PROFICIENCY IN ENGLISH

2

WITHOUT ANSWERS

AUTHENTIC EXAMINATION PAPERS FROM CAMBRIDGE ENGLISH LANGUAGE ASSESSMENT

Cambridge University Press
www.cambridge.org/elt

Cambridge English Language Assessment
www.cambridgeenglish.org

Information on this title: www.cambridge.org/9781107637924

First published 2015
Reprinted 2016

Printed in Dubai by Oriental Press

A catalogue record for this publication is available from the British Library

ISBN 978-1-107-63792-4 Student's Book without answers
ISBN 978-1-107-68693-9 Student's Book with answers
ISBN 978-1-107-64651-3 Student's Book with answers with audio
ISBN 978-1-107-64764-0 Audio CDs (2)

Contents

Thanks and acknowledgements

The authors and publishers acknowledge the following sources of copyright material and are grateful for the permissions granted. While every effort has been made, it has not always been possible to identify the sources of all the material used, or to trace all copyright holders. If any omissions are brought to our notice, we will be happy to include the appropriate acknowledgements on reprinting.

Text acknowledgements

New Scientist for the simplified extract on p. 10 'Mission to Mars', *New Scientist* 09/03/2013; for the re-written extract on p. 64 'The psychology of colour: Why winners wear red' by Daniel Elkan, *New Scientist* 28/08/2009; for the re-written extract on p. 68 'Stop the Rot' by James Mitchel Crow, *New Scientist* 19/06/2010; Guardian News and Media for the simplified extract on p. 14 'Blogging: the fine art of the confessional' by Scott Rosenberg, *The Guardian* 13/03/2011, for the simplified extract on p. 16 'Build it yourself at the UK's first bamboo bike workshop' by James Stewart, *The Guardian* 16/11/2012, for the adapted extract on p. 28 'A Life of their own' by Katharine Whitehorn, *The Observer* 30/09/2014, for the adapted extract on p. 39 'Forty years on, why we're still living in the moon's shadow' by Christopher Riley, *The Guardian* 22/12/2012, for the adapted extract on p. 45 'Here's a fresh slant on suburbia' by R. Moore, *Observer New Review* 24/02/2013, for the adapted extract on p. 51 'Without books, we would be very different people' by Gail Rebuck, *The Guardian* 31/12/2011, for the adapted extract on p. 59(A) 'Old music: Robert Wyatt – At Last I Am Free' by George Chesterton, *The Guardian* 10/01/2013, for the adapted extract on p. 59(B) 'Old music: Roy Harper – Another Day' by George Chesterton, *The Guardian* 28/06/2012, for the adapted extract on p. 59(C) 'Old music: Soft Cell – Say Hello Wave Goodbye' by Nick Hopkins, *The Guardian* 28/02/2013, for the adapted extract on p. 59(D) 'Old music: Rod Stewart – Maggie May' by Greg Freeman, *The Guardian* 18/10/2012, for the adapted extract on p. 59(E) 'Old music: Tom Waits – Martha' by Jon Lloyd, *The Guardian* 30/05/2012, for the adapted extract on p. 62 'Up Front, Prickly About Hedgehogs' by K Whitehorn, *The Guardian* 10/02/2013, for the simplified extract on p. 71 'How do we find time for what matters in the digital age?' by Tom Chatfield, *The Guardian* 26/01/2012, for the simplified extract on p. 76 'London Zoo's new Tiger Territory: built for the animals first, and visitors second?' by Oliver Wainwright, *The Guardian* 20/03/2013; Thomson Reuters for the simplified extract on p. 19 from 'How to study law' Bradney et al, *Sweet & Maxwell*, 1991. Reprinted with permission; National Public Radio, Inc for the simplified extract on p. 22 © 2013 National Public Radio, Inc. New Report titled "Monkey Calls Could Offer Clues For Origin Of Human Speech" was originally broadcast on NPR's All Things Considered on April 9, 2013, and is used with the permission of NPR. Any unauthorized duplication is strictly prohibited; Adapted extract on p. 23 from 'News Of The World: Kate Adie Interviewed On Music And War' by W Wallace, *The Quietus*, 07/03/2011. From News Of The World: Kate Adie Interviewed On Music And War by W Wallace with permission of Wyndham Wallace and Kate Adie Chief Correspondent, BBC News and author of Fighting on the Home Front: The Legacy of Women in World War 1. Hodder & Stoughton, 2013; ABC Radio National for the adapted extract on p. 25 from 'Remembering together' presented by Lynne Malcolm 27/05/2012. With permission; *The Independent* for the adapted extract on p. 31 'Journey to the Antartic Ocean' by Charlie Cooper, The Independent 26/09/12, for the adapted extract on p. 34 'Are you an Oscar or an Elmo' by Emily Jupp, *The Independent* 31/07/12, for the adapted extract on p. 54 'Manet and woman: Portraying life' by Adrian Hamilton, *The Independent* 22/01/13; Random House Group and Bill Bryson for the adapted extract on p. 36 from *Down Under* by Bill Bryson, *Black Swan*, 2010. Copyright © Bill Bryson, 2010. Reprinted with permission; Adapted extract on p. 42 from 'Elon Musk on Team Building, Warren Buffet and Mars' 09/02/2013. An evening with Elon Musk and Alison van Diggelen, 2013-01-22, CHM Lecture Collection, Lot X6753.2013, Digital Archive, Catalog Number 102746849, Computer History Museum with permission; CBA for the adapted extract on p. 42 from 'Viktor Mayer-Schönberger on forgetting in a digital age' 22/09/2009. *Spark* with Nora Young. Reprinted with permission; Rewritten extract on p. 44 from 'Feral animals in Australia', www.environment.gov.au/biodiversity/invasive/ferals/index.htm, licenced under a Creative Commons Attribution 3.0 Australia licence © Commonwealth of Australia 2013; Lonely Planet for the simplified extract on p. 56 'Lake Malawi's lost resort' by Marina Lewycka. Adapted with permission from Better than Fiction © 2012 Lonely Planet; Patrick Schwerdtfeger for the adapted extract on p. 62 from 'Go BIG!'. Reprinted with permission; The Sunday Times for the simplified extract on p. 74 'Kapow! It's Proust' by Robert Collins *The Sunday Times* 02/12/2012; The Open University and John Wiley & Sons for the adapted extract on p. 79 from 'Understanding Childhood' by Woodhead & Montgomery (eds), *The Open University/John Wiley & Sons*. Reprinted with permission; Teapigs for the rewritten extract on p. 82 'Teapigs – Clever Marketing By Tetley Tea' *Axel and Sophie Steenbergs Blog*. Post 06/2010 by Nick Kilby, Co-founder of Teapigs, with permission from www.teapigs.co.uk; ABC for the rewritten extract on p. 82 from a transcript of 'Cardboard, paper and play' presented by Antony Funnell. Reproduced by permission of the Australian Broadcasting Corporation (c) 2012 ABC. All rights reserved.

Photo acknowledgements

Test 1 Photo 1A C2: © Aurora Photos/Alamy; Test 1 Photo 1B C2: © Chris Linder/Visuals Unlimited/Corbis; Test 1 Photo 1C C2: © Sutton Images/Corbis; Test 2 Photo 2A C3: © Redlink/Corbis; Test 2 Photo 2B C3: © © Moodboard/Corbis; Test 2 Photo 2C C3: © Atlantide Phototravel/Corbis; Test 3 Photo 3A C4: © Jon Feingersh Photography Inc./Blend Images/Corbis; Test 3 Photo 3B C4: © Helen King/Corbis ; Test 3 Photo 3C C4: © Phil Boorman/cultura/Corbis; Test 3 Photo 3D C4: © Helen King/Corbis ; Test 4 Photo 4A C5: © Chad Ehlers/Alamy; Test 4 Photo 4B C5: © Atlantide Phototravel/Corbis.

The recordings which accompany this book were made at dsound, London.

Introduction

This collection of four complete practice tests comprises papers from the Cambridge English: Proficiency (CPE) examination; students can practise with these tests on their own or with the help of a teacher.

The CPE examination is part of a suite of general English examinations produced by Cambridge English Language Assessment. This suite consists of five examinations that have similar characteristics but are designed for different levels of English language ability. Within the five levels, CPE is at Level C2 in the Council of Europe's *Common European Framework of Reference for Languages: Learning, teaching, assessment*. It has been accredited by Ofqual, the statutory regulatory authority in England, at Level 3 in the National Qualifications Framework. CPE is recognised by universities, employers, governments and other organisations around the world as proof of the ability to use English to function at the highest levels of academic and professional life.

Examination	Council of Europe Framework Level	UK National Qualifications Framework Level
Cambridge English: Proficiency *Certificate of Proficiency in English (CPE)*	C2	3
Cambridge English: Advanced *Certificate in Advanced English (CAE)*	C1	2
Cambridge English: First *First Certificate in English (FCE)*	B2	1
Cambridge English: Preliminary *Preliminary English Test (PET)*	B1	Entry 3
Cambridge English: Key *Key English Test (KET)*	A2	Entry 2

Further information

The information contained in this practice book is designed to be an overview of the exam. For a full description of all of the above exams including information about task types, testing focus and preparation, please see the relevant handbooks which can be obtained from Cambridge English Language Assessment at the address below or from the website at: www.cambridgeenglish.org

Cambridge English Language Assessment
1 Hills Road
Cambridge CB1 2EU
United Kingdom

Telephone: +44 1223 553997
Fax: +44 1223 553621
e-mail: helpdesk@cambridgeenglish.org

The structure of CPE: an overview

The CPE examination consists of four papers:

Reading and Use of English 1 hour 30 minutes
This paper consists of seven parts with 53 questions. For Parts 1 to 4, the test contains texts with accompanying grammar and vocabulary tasks, and discrete items with a grammar and vocabulary focus. For Parts 5 to 7, the test contains texts and accompanying reading comprehension tasks.

Writing 1 hour 30 minutes
This paper consists of two parts which carry equal marks. In Part 1, which is compulsory, candidates must write an essay with a discursive focus of between 240 and 280 words. The task requires candidates to summarise and evaluate the key ideas contained in two texts of approximately 100 words each.

In Part 2, there are five questions from which candidates must choose one to write about. The range of tasks from which questions may be drawn includes an article, a letter, a report, a review, and an essay (set text questions only). The last question (Question 5) is based on the set texts. These set texts remain on the list for two years. Look on the website, or contact the Cambridge English Language Assessment Centre Exams Manager in your area for the up-to-date list of set texts. Question 5 has two options from which candidates choose one to write about. In this part, candidates write between 280 and 320 words.

Assessment is based on the Assessment Scales, comprising four subscales: Content, Communicative Achievement, Organisation, and Language.

Listening 40 minutes (approximately)
This paper consists of four parts with 30 questions. Each part contains a recorded text or texts and corresponding comprehension tasks. Each part is heard twice.

Speaking 16 minutes
The Speaking test consists of three parts. The standard test format is two candidates and two examiners. One examiner acts as interlocutor and manages the interaction either by asking questions or providing cues for the candidates. The other acts as assessor and does not join in the conversation. The test consists of short exchanges with the interlocutor, a collaborative task involving both candidates and an individual long turn followed by a three-way discussion.

Grading
The overall CPE grade is based on the total score gained in all four papers. All candidates receive a Statement of Results which includes a graphical profile of their performance in all four skills and Use of English. Certificates are given

to candidates who pass the examination with grade A, B or C. Candidates whose performance is below C2 level, but falls within Level C1, receive a Cambridge English certificate stating they have demonstrated ability at C1 level. Candidates whose performance falls below Level C1 do not receive a certificate.

For further information on grading and results, go to the Cambridge English Language Assessment website (see page 5).

Test 1

READING AND USE OF ENGLISH (1 hour 30 minutes)

Part 1

For questions **1–8**, read the text below and decide which answer (**A**, **B**, **C** or **D**) best fits each gap.

Mark your answers **on the separate answer sheet.**

There is an example at the beginning (**0**).

0	**A** disagreement	**B** dissent	**C** dispute	**D** discord

0	A	B	C	D
	▭	▭	▬	▭

England's breakfast revolution

The importance of a good breakfast is beyond **(0)** .... according to health experts, but in historical terms breakfast is a relatively new arrival in England, with descriptions of breakfast seldom **(1)** .... in medieval literature. **(2)** ...., there are scattered references to travellers having a meal at dawn before **(3)** .... on arduous journeys, and to the sick sitting down to breakfast for medicinal reasons, but most people went without unless they were monarchs or nobles.

However, in the sixteenth century it gradually became the **(4)** ...., not the exception. Some writers have **(5)** .... this to the greater availability of food. Proponents of this view have not always considered other profound social changes. For example, new **(6)** .... of employment may well offer a plausible explanation for the greater importance now **(7)** .... to breakfast, as individuals were increasingly employed for a prescribed number of hours. Often this involved starting work extremely early. Thus, having a meal first thing in the morning was **(8)** .... in necessity, and was no longer associated with social status alone.

	A	B	C	D
1	**A** displaying	**B** manifesting	**C** disclosing	**D** featuring
2	**A** Deservedly	**B** Admittedly	**C** Conceivably	**D** Assuredly
3	**A** engaging	**B** launching	**C** embarking	**D** committing
4	**A** norm	**B** prototype	**C** standard	**D** trait
5	**A** attributed	**B** assigned	**C** accounted	**D** accorded
6	**A** figures	**B** shapes	**C** lines	**D** patterns
7	**A** linked	**B** fixed	**C** attached	**D** secured
8	**A** embedded	**B** rooted	**C** entrenched	**D** founded

Part 2

For questions **9–16**, read the text below and think of the word which best fits each space. Use only **one** word in each space. There is an example at the beginning **(0)**. Write your answers **IN CAPITAL LETTERS on the separate answer sheet.**

Example: | **0** | F | O | R |

Mission to Mars

Wanted: a middle-aged, married couple **(0)** .... a 501-day round trip to Mars. Applicants must be physically and emotionally robust.

This will be the profile of the very first Martian astronauts if multi-millionaire Dennis Tito's plans to launch a capsule on 5 January 2018 actually **(9)** .... to fruition. The capsule will take the crew to about 160 km above Mars. The spacecraft will use the gravity of Mars to allow it to return to Earth without burning any more fuel, for fuel efficiency is a priority – the 2018 deadline has been fixed **(10)** .... the next launch window when Mars and Earth align again isn't **(11)** .... 2031. It's a **(12)** .... order, but the race is on to develop systems involving totally new technologies. **(13)** .... that these can be put in place soon enough, the spacecraft might just **(14)** .... it. But even if it **(15)** .... leaves Earth, the efforts to achieve these ambitious goals will not be in **(16)** ...., as they will lead to valuable advances for future missions.

Part 3

For questions **17–24**, read the text below. Use the word given in capitals at the end of some of the lines to form a word that fits in the space in the same line. There is an example at the beginning (**0**). tWrite your answers **IN CAPITAL LETTERS on the separate answer sheet.**

Example: | **0** | T | E | N | D | E | N | C | Y |

CRYING

Charles Darwin thought that the human **(0)** .... to cry had no obvious	**TEND**
(17) .... purpose. He was almost certainly wrong. More recently scientists have	**EVOLVE**
pointed to its social **(18)** ...., with psychiatrist John Bowlby highlighting the role	**SIGN**
of crying in developing the **(19)** .... between mother and child. Many believe	**ATTACH**
that tears, at least during childhood, are mainly an expression of **(20)**	**HELP**
However, the persistence of crying into adulthood is harder to explain. It seems	
that the sound of crying becomes considerably less important than the visual	
signal it conveys. It may have been **(21)** .... to early human communities as a	**ADVANTAGE**
means of promoting trust and social connectedness.	
Tears can undoubtedly have other causes too. We may cry to express sympathy	
for those suffering terrible **(22)** .... Furthermore, tears can be shed	**JUST**
(23) ...., rather to our embarrassment, when we hear inspiring music or moving	**VOLUNTARY**
speeches. We may cry when watching a sentimental film, but interestingly, this is	
more likely to occur in company than when we are alone. The social function of	
crying would seem to be **(24)** ...., but research continues.	**DENY**

Part 4

For questions **25–30**, complete the second sentence so that it has a similar meaning to the first sentence, using the word given. **Do not change the word given**. You must use between **three** and **eight** words, including the word given. Here is an example (**0**).

Example:

0 Do you mind if I watch you while you paint?

objection

Do you .... you while you paint?

0	have any objection to my watching

Write **only** the missing words **on the separate answer sheet**.

---

25 I hope the committee will consider this new information when they meet next week.

account

I hope this new information .... when the committee meet next week.

26 James did not find it difficult to answer the interviewer's questions.

coming

James had no .... the interviewer's questions.

27 The more experienced members of the expedition were made responsible for finding food.

charge

The more experienced members of the expedition .... finding food.

28 The agent said he no longer thought that Sam Bowker would ever appear in a Hollywood film.

hope

The agent said he .... appearing in a Hollywood film.

29 My father said that the portrait did not look like him.

resemblence

My father said that the portrait .... him.

30 Leo doesn't understand why his sister is opposing his plan.

what

Leo doesn't understand .... his plan is.

Part 5

You are going to read an article about the history of blogging. For questions **31–36**, choose the answer (**A**, **B**, **C** or **D**) which you think fits best according to the text. Mark your answers **on the separate answer sheet**.

Blogging: Confessing to the world

Some time ago, a website highlighted the risks of public check-ins – online announcements of your whereabouts. The site's point was blunt: you may think you are just telling the world, 'Hey, I'm at this place' – but you are also advertising your out-and-about-ness to all kinds of people everywhere – not all of them people you might like to bump into. This appeared to confirm the growing awareness that there might be a downside to all the frantic sharing the web has enabled. The vast new opportunities to publish any and every aspect of our lives to a potentially global audience hold out all sorts of tantalising possibilities: Wealth! Fame! So we plunge into the maelstrom of the internet, tossing confessions, personal photos and stories into the digital vortex. Too late we realise that the water is crowded and treacherous – and we are lost.

Depressing? Perhaps, but don't give up. This future has a map, drawn for us years ago by a reckless group of online pioneers. In the early days of the web, they sailed these waters and located all the treacherous shoals. They got fired from their jobs, found and lost friends and navigated celebrity's temptations and perils – all long before the invention of social networking. These pioneers, the first wave of what we now call bloggers, have already been where the rest of us seem to be going. Before their tales scroll off our collective screen, it's worth spending a little time with them. After all, those who cannot learn from history are doomed to repost it.

In January 1994, Justin Hall, a 19-year-old student, began posting to the 'WWW', as it was then known, something inhabited mostly by grad students, scientists and a handful of precocious teens like him. The web had been invented at CERN, the international physics lab in Switzerland, so researchers could more easily share their work. Hall saw something else: an opportunity to share his life. Link by link, he built a hypertext edifice of autobiography, a dense thicket of verbal self-exposure leavened with photos and art. In January 1996, on a dare, he began posting a daily blog, and readers flocked to the spectacle of a reckless young man pushing the boundaries of this new medium in every direction at once.

Hall's ethos was absolute: cross his path and you could appear on his site; no topic was taboo. Certainly, this was the work of an exhibitionist, but there was also a rigour and beauty to his project that only a snob would refuse to call art. One day though, visitors to Hall's site discovered his home page gone, replaced with a single anguished video titled *Dark Night*. His story tumbled out; he'd fallen spectacularly in love, but when he started writing about it on his site he was told 'either the blog goes, or I do'. He'd published his life on the internet and, Hall protested, 'it makes people not trust me'. The blog went, but the dilemma persists. Sharing online is great. But if you expect your song of yourself to 'make people want to be with you', you'll be disappointed.

In 2002, Heather Armstrong, a young web worker in Los Angeles, had a blog called Dooce. Occasionally, she wrote about her job at a software company. One day an anonymous colleague sent the address of Armstrong's blog to every vice president at her company – including some whom she'd mocked – and that was the end of her job. Those who study the peculiar social patterns of the networked world have a term to describe what was at work here. They call it the 'online distribution effect': that feeling so many of us have that we can get away with saying things online that we'd never dream of saying in person. But our digital lives are interwoven with our real lives. When we pretend otherwise, we risk making terrible, life-changing mistakes.

Armstrong's saga had a happy ending. Though she was upset by the experience and stopped blogging for several months afterwards, she ended up getting married and restarting her blog with a focus on her new family. Today she is a star in the burgeoning ranks of 'mommy bloggers' and her writing supports her house hold. Once a poster child for the wages of web indiscretion, she has become a virtuoso of managed self-revelation. What Armstrong has figured out is something we would all do well to remember: the web may allow us to say anything, but that doesn't mean we should.

31 Why does the writer describe a website about public check-ins in the first paragraph?

A to reinforce the concerns already felt by some people
B to remind readers to beware of false promises
C to explain that such sites often have a hidden agenda
D to show that the risks of internet use are sometimes overestimated

32 What is the writer's attitude to the online pioneers mentioned in the second paragraph?

A He is concerned by the risks they took.
B He appreciates their unprecedented achievements.
C He admires their technical skills.
D He is impressed by the extent of their cooperation.

33 What does the writer suggest about Justin Hall in the third paragraph?

A He was unusually innovative in his approach.
B His work was popular for the wrong reasons.
C He inspired others writing in different fields of study.
D His work displayed considerable literary skill.

34 What point is exemplified by the references to Hall's project in the fourth paragraph?

A People usually dislike exhibitionists.
B Someone's life can be a form of art.
C Relationships are always a private matter.
D Being too open may be counterproductive.

35 What does the account of Armstrong's later career suggest about blogging?

A It is important to choose an appropriate audience.
B It is possible to blog safely and successfully.
C It is vital to consider the feelings of others.
D It is best to avoid controversial subjects when blogging.

36 In this article, the writer's aim is to

A illustrate a point.
B defend a proposition.
C describe developments.
D compare arguments.

Part 6

You are going to read an article about a company which makes unusual bicycles. Seven paragraphs have been removed from the extract. Choose from the paragraphs **A–H** the one which fits each gap (**37–43**). There is one extra paragraph which you do not need to use. Mark your answers **on the separate answer sheet**.

Build it yourself at the UK's first bamboo bike workshop

A course at the Bamboo Bike Club, run by engineers James Marr and Ian McMillan, buys you a computer-designed custom frame plus a fun weekend of bike-building

It's Saturday morning in Hackney Wick, east London, and apart from a mechanic deep in the bowels of a truck, the only sign of life among the small factories on a backstreet is a whine of machinery from an upper window – work has begun at Bamboo Bike Club, Britain's only bamboo bike-building course. I've gone along to watch the action.

37

There's a sense of energy and industry. And of fun. Woodwork class was never like this. Bamboo is one of the most interesting trends to emerge in bike construction. Names like Californian manufacturer Calfee Design or Yorkshire's Bamboo Bikes have revived a construction method pioneered as early as 1894. The problem for most cyclists is the price. A ready-made bamboo frame from these companies retails for $2,995, or £1,868.

38

Only after they had refined their research into a marketable product – James now tosses out phrases like 'close-noded thick-wall tubes' while talking about bamboo – did they realise they were on the wrong track. 'We realised we didn't want just to sell frames. We wanted to share the joy of making something; the craft of creating something unique and sustainable,' James explains.

39

The question for me, a king of the botch job – my terrible handiwork failures litter my house – was about quality. On day one, the boys explain how to select bamboo for strength and how to form strong joints before tubes are glued lightly in place in the workshop: first the front triangle composed of 40 mm diameter bamboo; then the thinner, more fiddly seat and the chain assembly. Alloy tubes are inserted for the handlebars, wheel forks and other parts which require the strength and precise engineering impossible in bamboo.

40

James and Ian buzz cheerfully between workbenches, supervising every cut, triple-checking every joint, and will take over if a task seems insurmountable. The self-build is half the attraction for most participants; it may be no coincidence that all those on this course were engineers. For the rest of us, Ian reassures that everyone messes up once or twice.

41

Sunday is a more relaxed day, mainly spent building the lugs. Or rather, wraps: hemp bindings wrapped around the joints and dropouts then glued with epoxy resin to form a strong bond that disperses loads evenly throughout the frame. With a final polymer coating for waterproofing, the bike is ready for wheels, brakes, gears, saddle and any other individual touches. And it is a bike built for the long haul, just as strong, the pair claim, as its metal equivalents.

42

Technical issues aside, how good does a bamboo bike look? Somewhat scruffy alongside professional frames, it turns out – the hemp weave can look a bit like parcel tape, for example. But there's no denying their individuality and that, say James and Ian, is the point.

43

They also cycle well. I take James's bike for a spin and the ride is light, stiff and smooth thanks to bamboo's ability to dampen vibration. Impressive, considering I target every pothole. 'Some people love the build, but for me these workshops come together when the bike is on the road,' James says. 'They're so light, so effortless to ride. So much fun to ride too – take a Harley-style retro bike, add 10 and you're still not close.' And the price? Less than £500.

A All this, together with the technical skill involved in using jigs, power tools and design blueprints, is a leap of faith for someone whose idea of DIY is flatpack furniture assembly. Accurate cutting for a clean joint can be tricky, for example.

B Personally though, I believe that any bicycle made from this kind of material should be a relaxed affair, something for cruising sedately around on rather than racing. I therefore plump for a frame that avoids the stiff angularity of my existing metal machine: a 'Classic English' giving a gentle, easy- going ride.

C Frames have been set up for the three custom bikes under construction. Bamboo has been selected from a stockpile. Now crossbars and seatposts are being cut according to the lengths specified on each design's blueprint.

D No problem – just get another piece and have another go. Such is the benefit of bamboo. Each length has been pre-checked for quality, so you get to indulge in frame aesthetics: plain bamboo, black or mottled.

E If Calfee and their like are safe, middle-of-the-road rock, then Bamboo Bike Club are the punks, the rebels; less up against the big names than creating bikes that embody the DIY spirit and that will engender more passion than the average factory-line model.

F It was this, plus the design challenge, that led James and Ian to spend years cooped up in a shed in Brecon, Wales. Their idea was to establish a boutique bamboo bike business with products within reach of the average cyclist.

G Ian has ridden his for over a year on a 16-mile commute, while James has failed to destroy one bike off-road over three months of testing. 'To be honest, our bikes are over-engineered – we use larger diameter tubes and over-thick bindings – but I prefer it like that,' James says.

H The outcome was something more community than company, and as such, the Bamboo Bike Club is still an occupation sandwiched between full-time jobs – James makes wind turbines and Ian is a civil engineer. But they seem to be on the right track, with monthly courses whose competitive price buys you a computer-designed custom bike frame plus a fun weekend of bike-building.

Part 7

You are going to read extracts from an introductory book about studying the law. For questions **44–53**, choose from the sections (**A–D**). The extracts may be chosen more than once. Mark your answers **on the separate answer sheet.**

In which extract are the following mentioned?

the relative frequency of certain types of legal cases	44	
input by those who are not directly involved in a dispute	45	
how common transactions assume certain guarantees	46	
ascertaining the effectiveness of a legal system	47	
determining the consequences of altering the legal system	48	
the influence of popular depictions of the law	49	
a reluctance to submit to formal legal processes	50	
how a decentralised legal system depends on a feeling of reciprocity	51	
the lack of drama in the way the law operates	52	
the absence of a certain type of legal institution	53	

Studying the law

A

Ordinary people regularly encounter law in a variety of circumstances. Freely-negotiated commercial contracts may bind them to act in particular ways. By becoming members of a sports club or a trade union they agree to comply with a set of rules. Sometimes these forms of law will use the courts to enforce their arrangements. In other cases privately-instituted adjudication bodies are established, a third party being appointed to decide whether an agreement or rule has been broken or not. These kinds of arrangements may seem very different from the normal idea of law, especially if law is thought of mainly in terms of the criminal law. However, it is possible to see law simply as a way of regulating our actions, of deciding what can be done and what cannot be done. Most laws are not about something spectacular but, rather, about the details of ordinary life. Every time a purchase is made, a contract is made. Both parties make promises about what they will do; one to hand over the goods, one to pay the price. In this and other ways, everybody is involved in law every day of their lives.

B

Legal rules can be divided up in many different ways. The rules show differences in purpose, in origin and form, in the consequences when they are breached, and in matters of procedure, remedies and enforcement. One of the most fundamental divisions in law is the division between criminal and civil law. Newcomers to the study of law tend to assume that criminal law occupies the bulk of a lawyer's caseload and of a law student's studies. This is an interesting by-product of the portrayal of the legal system by the media. Criminal law weighs very lightly in terms of volume when measured against non-criminal (that is, civil) law. There are more rules of civil law than there are of criminal law; more court cases involve breach of the civil law than that of the criminal law.

C

The term 'national law' is used to mean the internal legal rules of a particular country, in contrast to international law which deals with the external relationships of a state with other states. There is no world government or legislature issuing and enforcing laws to which all nations are subject. The international legal order has no single governing body and operates by agreement between states. This means that the creation, interpretation and enforcement of international law lie primarily in the hands of states themselves. Its scope and effectiveness depend on the sense of mutual benefit and obligation involved in adhering to the rules. Disputes about the scope and interpretation of international law are rarely resolved by the use of international courts or binding arbitration procedures of an international organisation. This is because submission to an international court or similar process is entirely voluntary and few states are likely to agree to this if there is a serious risk of losing their case or where important political or national interests are at stake.

D

One source of detailed information about the legal system is statistical analyses. Information about the number of cases handled by a court shows in specific terms what a court's workload is. Changes in these from year to year may indicate some effects of changes in the law and practice. Statistical tests can establish that there is a relationship, a correlation, between different things. For example, the length of a sentence for theft may correlate with the value of the items stolen or the experience of the judge who heard the case. This means that the sentence will be longer if, for example, more items are stolen or the judge is more experienced. A correlation can provide evidence for a theory. Such confirmation is important; without it we have little to establish the impact the law has, being forced to rely on individual instances of its application and having to assume that these have general truth. Empirical study of the operation of law may reveal areas of improvement. It can also confirm that, measured by particular standards, the courts are working well.

WRITING (1 hour 30 minutes)

Part 1

Read the two texts below.

Write an essay summarising and evaluating the key points from both texts. Use your own words throughout as far as possible, and include your own ideas in your answers.

Write your answer in **240–280** words.

1

Throwing things away

Every week many of us throw away a huge amount of stuff, ranging from packaging for food and plastic bottles to old newspapers and junk mail. Fortunately some, though not all, of this can be recycled successfully and both governments and private citizens seem to be doing their best to ensure that this happens nowadays. We should be careful not to congratulate ourselves too soon, however, because whether enough is being done is highly debatable. For example, the vast numbers of plastic bags used, many of which are not biodegradable, damage the environment, most notably the oceans, where they endanger marine life.

Communications technology

It seems that nowadays we keep electronic products such as mobile phones for only a short time, because we are bombarded with highly effective advertising that persuades us that we need to discard our present model in favour of the latest, improved device. Our willingness to discard such products may also be a consequence of the dizzying pace of technological change. We can hardly be expected to be content to remain behind the times, and we naturally wish to keep up with the latest exciting features and developments in communications technology.

Write your **essay**.

Part 2

Write an answer to **one** of the questions **2–5** in this part. Write your answer in **280–320** words in an appropriate style.

---

2 A general interest magazine has recently published a feature entitled 'Taking risks makes life worth living'. The editor has asked readers to write in with their own experiences and views on the topic. You decide to write a letter briefly describing a risk you once took and its consequences. You should also discuss why some people are particularly attracted to taking risks and how this behaviour might be justified.

Write your **letter**.

3 Some bus services in your area are to be withdrawn, and the local council has asked people to submit reports for the council website on the impact this will have. You decide to submit a report on one bus service that is under consideration. Your report should briefly describe the route and explain its importance. You should also assess the role that a good transport system plays in either urban or rural areas.

Write your **report**.

4 A magazine is running a series of articles on people's experiences of being close to nature, for example, visits to beautiful lakes or mountains, or encounters with wildlife. You decide to write an article in which you briefly describe an experience you have had when you were close to nature, and explain what you learned from this. You should also evaluate the role that contact with nature plays in people's lives.

Write your **article**.

5 Write an answer to **one** of the following two questions based on **one** of the titles below. Write **5(a)** or **5(b)** at the beginning of your answer.

(a) Anne Tyler: *The Accidental Tourist*
'Two of the most important influences in this book are a child we never meet – and a dog.' Write a review for your local college magazine of *The Accidental Tourist*. You should briefly explain this comment and analyse the roles of Ethan and Edward in the story as a whole.

Write your **review**.

(b) Ann Patchett: *Bel Canto*
An international literary magazine has asked readers to send in articles entitled 'Music is the food of love … ' with reference to the role of music in books they have read.

You decide to write an article about *Bel Canto*, briefly describing Roxanne's role in the house and evaluating the connection between music and love in her relationships.

Write your **article**.

LISTENING (40 minutes approximately)

Part 1

You will hear three different extracts.

For questions **1–6**, choose the answer (**A**, **B** or **C**) which fits best according to what you hear. There are two questions for each extract.

Extract One

You hear two colleagues discussing the work they are doing in a historic palace.

1 What is the man's role in the restoration work?

- **A** managing the restoration being done
- **B** researching how previous restoration was done
- **C** assessing whether restoration needs to be done

2 How does the woman feel now about the purchase of an original dining table?

- **A** impressed it was worth so much
- **B** frustrated that it took so long to find it
- **C** satisfied with the part she played

Extract Two

You hear part of an interview with a scientist who is talking about her research into primate communication.

3 The scientist compares the sounds primates make to human speech in order to illustrate

- **A** the research methods scientists have used.
- **B** a question scientists have been trying to solve.
- **C** the huge variety in primate sounds.

4 The scientist thinks the reason that gelada monkeys are significant is because

- **A** they use facial gestures in a similar way to humans.
- **B** the types of sounds they make are similar to human speech.
- **C** the rhythm of their vocalisation is similar to that of humans.

Extract Three

You hear a journalist talking about changes that have taken place over her professional lifetime.

5 What explanation does the journalist give for changes in the quality of news reports?

- **A** the ease with which information can be manipulated
- **B** the public demand for sensational images
- **C** the value placed on real-time reporting

6 She refers to different ways of eating to suggest that readers of printed newspapers

- **A** begin by selecting what interests them most.
- **B** tackle content that is difficult.
- **C** skim over the majority of topics.

Part 2

You will hear part of a lecture about an architect called Josh Keysall, who became famous for designing environmentally friendly houses known as Earthpods.

For questions **7–15**, complete the sentences with a word or short phrase.

Soon after graduating, Keysall thought up a successful way of providing **(7)** .... in the construction of buildings.

In his first Earthpod, Keysall used **(8)** .... instead of bricks to make the walls.

The speaker says the Earthpods are passive solar buildings with walls which are like **(9)** .... in the way they function.

Keysall uses the term **(10)** .... to describe the independence of his Earthpods from conventional energy sources.

An Earthpod originally used as a **(11)** .... in Switzerland was specially adapted for the climate.

In Belgium, safety regulations prevented Keysall from using **(12)** .... to construct an Earthpod.

In the UK, an Earthpod project involved the protection of some **(13)** .... living in the area.

Following complaints about defects such as **(14)** ...., Keysall lost his professional status.

A film called **(15)** .... has been made about Keysall's life, work and legal battles.

Part 3

You will hear part of an interview in which two academics, Julia Ford and Stuart Cameron, discuss human memory.

For questions **16–20**, choose the answer (**A**, **B**, **C** or **D**) which fits best according to what you hear.

---

16 Julia and Stuart both think that concerns about the reliability of shared memories are

A over-emphasised in some studies.
B reasonable in some situations.
C underestimated by some psychologists.
D unfounded in legal contexts.

17 What surprised Stuart about how older couples remembered information?

A the marked difference in the success of their approach
B the few signs of personal disagreement
C the great variety in the memories recalled
D the evidence of the use of similar processes.

18 Julia and Stuart agree that the least effective sharing of memories occurred when one person

A ignored the knowledge of the other person.
B tried to control the direction of the conversation.
C knew a lot more about the topic than the other person.
D contradicted information given by the other person.

19 Julia contrasts humans with animals in order to

A illustrate human social independence.
B suggest humans abuse their privileges.
C emphasise the carelessness of some humans.
D explain how humans are vulnerable.

20 When talking about the nature of change in human memory, Julia and Stuart reveal

A their respect for art history.
B their insistence on scientific evidence.
C their interest in cultural explanations.
D their differences regarding philosophical claims.

Part 4

You will hear five short extracts in which university students are talking about the profession they are training for.

TASK ONE

For questions **21–25**, choose from the list (**A–H**) how each speaker feels about their course.

TASK TWO

For questions **26–30**, choose from the list (**A–H**) what each speaker says about future prospects for those on the course.

While you listen, you must complete both tasks.

Task One

A appreciative of its challenge
B worried about falling behind with the practical aspects
C surprised by its wider relevance
D frustrated at the lack of information
E pleased at having overcome a problem
F surprised at changes that have taken place
G pleased with progress relative to others
H concerned by the lack of support for others

Speaker	Answer	Question
Speaker 1		**21**
Speaker 2		**22**
Speaker 3		**23**
Speaker 4		**24**
Speaker 5		**25**

Task Two

A Success is easier for those with good connections.
B A good reputation can count for a lot.
C Related work may be difficult to find.
D The job market is expected to grow in this area.
E A personal quality is needed that many lack.
F To get a well-paid position it is necessary to specialise.
G Academic success is vital.
H The first years of work are very stressful.

Speaker	Answer	Question
Speaker 1		**26**
Speaker 2		**27**
Speaker 3		**28**
Speaker 4		**29**
Speaker 5		**30**

SPEAKING (16 minutes)

There are two examiners. One (the interlocutor) conducts the test, providing you with the necessary materials and explaining what you have to do. The other examiner (the assessor) will be introduced to you, but then takes no further part in the interaction.

Part 1 (2 minutes)

The interlocutor first asks you and your partner a few questions which focus on information about yourselves.

Part 2 (4 minutes)

In this part of the test you and your partner are asked to talk together. The interlocutor places a set of pictures on the table in front of you. There may be only one picture in the set or as many as seven pictures. This stimulus provides the basis for a discussion. The interlocutor first asks an introductory question which focuses on two of the pictures (or in the case of a single picture, on aspects of the picture). After about a minute, the interlocutor gives you both a decision-making task based on the same set of pictures.

The pictures for Part 2 are on page C2 of the colour section.

Part 3 (10 minutes)

You are each given the opportunity to talk for two minutes, to comment after your partner has spoken and to take part in a more general discussion.

The interlocutor gives you a card with a question written on it and asks you to talk about it for two minutes. After you have spoken, the interlocutor asks you both another question related to the topic on the card, addressing your partner first. This procedure is repeated, so that your partner receives a card and speaks for two minutes and a follow-up question is asked.

Finally, the interlocutor asks some further questions, which lead to a discussion on a general theme related to the subjects already covered in Part 3.

The cards for Part 3 are on pages C6–C7 of the colour section.

Test 2

READING AND USE OF ENGLISH (1 hour 30 minutes)

Part 1

For questions **1–8**, read the text below and decide which answer (**A**, **B**, **C** or **D**) best fits each gap.

Mark your answers **on the separate answer sheet.**

There is an example at the beginning (**0**).

Example:

0	**A**	distinguish	**B**	sense	**C**	feel	**D**	identify

0	A	B	C	D
	▭	▬	▭	▭

The way we see the things around us

'Pastry,' once wrote a cookery expert, 'like horses and children, seems to **(0)** .... if you are afraid of it and plays up **(1)** ....' Had she been writing today, she might well have mentioned that computers are just the same. Like small children, they do not **(2)** .... well to force, and just as one way of **(3)** .... with a fractious child is to send it to its room to **(4)** .... off, so quite often, if the machine is giving trouble, the first thing to try is simply switching it off and doing something else; quite why the machine works **(5)** .... when you boot it up again I have no idea.

(6) .... human emotions and feelings to inanimate objects is, of course, extremely unscientific; it's only those who don't understand machines who believe that they behave like people. But I would **(7)** .... that, although treating machines like people may be misguided, it is **(8)** ...., in general, to treating people like machines.

	A	B	C	D
1	correspondingly	similarly	accordingly	appropriately
2	respond	reply	adapt	answer
3	reacting	dealing	handling	bargaining
4	ease	calm	quieten	cool
5	perfectly	completely	reasonably	competently
6	Associating	Attributing	Accrediting	Admitting
7	support	decide	confirm	maintain
8	desirable	preferable	advisable	suitable

Part 2

For questions **9–16**, read the text below and think of the word which best fits each space. Use only **one** word in each space. There is an example at the beginning (**0**). Write your answers **IN CAPITAL LETTERS on the separate answer sheet.**

Example: | **0** | A | W | A | Y |

Driverless cars

Driverless cars would of course, do **(0)** .... with the stress of driving, allowing their occupants to read, browse the internet or take a nap, and they would also eliminate accidents caused by human error.

The benefits would go **(9)** .... comfort and safety, however, since they would also revolutionise transport and urban planning. Traffic lights and road signs would no **(10)** .... be needed. Different autonomous vehicles on the road would be able to coordinate their movements, and travel **(11)** .... close formation, so that traffic would be kept flowing without interruption, **(12)** .... journeys quicker and road use more efficient. On the one hand, this might mean that cities got bigger, as a **(13)** .... of commuting times being reduced; on the **(14)** ...., they could become denser, with houses in the space previously dedicated to roads.

It may all sound **(15)** .... science fiction, but much of the technology needed to turn ordinary vehicles into self-driving ones already exists. Almost **(16)** .... car makers are developing systems which will in effect turn cars into autonomous robots.

Part 3

For questions **17–24**, read the text below. Use the word given in capitals at the end of some of the lines to form a word that fits in the space in the same line. There is an example at the beginning (**0**). Write your answers **IN CAPITAL LETTERS on the separate answer sheet**.

Example: **0** M I C R O S C O P I C

Exploring the oceans

A million new species of **(0)** .... sea life have recently been observed for	**SCOPE**
the first time, promising **(17)** .... about the marine ecosystem that could	**REVEAL**
(18) .... our understanding of the impact of climate change on the oceans.	**REVOLVE**
Each new life form was observed in the **(19)** .... of the Pacific and Atlantic	**DEEP**
oceans by the research vessel, the *Tara*, which was a **(20)** .... small ship to be	**COMPARE**
undertaking a mission on this scale.	
The expedition's **(21)** .... show for the first time the quite remarkable diversity	**FIND**
of tiny plankton that are a vital food source for fish and whales. In total, 1.5 million	
species of microorganisms were recorded – **(22)** .... more than previously	**SIGNIFY**
thought – and some of these were extraordinarily beautiful.	
Worryingly, the scientists report that the oceans are becoming more acidic, and	
this will continue if **(23)** .... of carbon dioxide increase, or even if they remain	**EMIT**
at current levels. Since these organisms are sensitive to acid, they could become	
(24) .... species in the future.	**DANGER**

Part 4

For questions **25–30**, complete the second sentence so that it has a similar meaning to the first sentence, using the word given. **Do not change the word given**. You must use between **three** and **eight** words, including the word given. Here is an example (**0**).

Example:

0 Do you mind if I watch you while you paint?

objection

Do you .... you while you paint?

0	have any objection to my watching

Write **only** the missing words **on the separate answer sheet**.

---

25 Sam moved house only because he disliked commuting.

dislike

But for his .... moved house.

26 Katy didn't seem nervous, even though she was making her speech without notes.

sign

Katy ...., even though she was making her speech without notes.

27 The manager said he was extremely confident that his team could cope with the challenges ahead.

every

The manager said he .... to cope with the challenges ahead.

28 More and more tourists are visiting the ancient towns in the mountains.

growth

There .... tourists visiting the ancient towns in the mountains.

29 I don't think Harriet has any idea how difficult it is to use this apparatus.

involved

I don't think Harriet has any idea .... this apparatus.

30 Because the room is not available today, they have rearranged the meeting for next week.

put

Because the room is not available today, the meeting .... next week.

Part 5

You are going to read an article about the advantages and disadvantages of pessimistic and optimistic attitudes. For questions **31–36**, choose the answer (**A**, **B**, **C** or **D**) which you think fits best according to the text. Mark your answers **on the separate answer sheet.**

Are you an Optimist or a Pessimist?

Whichever you are, a new book reveals that you can learn a lot from attempting the opposite attitude.

As a nation, the British are not a very optimistic bunch. When we were first granted the honour of hosting the 2012 Olympic Games, according to an opinion poll at the time, 55 per cent of us were more concerned about the likely impact on the transport network while the Games were on than with celebrating the arrival of the greatest show on Earth. But alongside this type of staunch pessimism resides an unsettling feeling that we should be more positive. We are always trying to dislodge each other's pessimism. Test it for yourself: sit gloomily in a public place and see how long it takes before a smiling passer-by says, 'Cheer up, it might never happen!' or offers one of those trite aphorisms about 'looking on the bright side' or 'clouds having silver linings'.

The self-help industry rakes in billions through peddling hope and positive thinking. But can a positive outlook really improve our lives? How can optimism make people more trustworthy, or sports events more successful? It can't, says Professor Elaine Fox, a neuroscientist who recently published a book called *Rainy Brain, Sunny Brain* about our ambivalent feelings of optimism and pessimism. Our negativity is the response of a rational mind and positivity is a delusion, she says, and for most of us they both act to balance us out. 'Positivity is a delusion. But it is a useful delusion. If we didn't have some sort of optimism we wouldn't ever get out of bed in the morning. But pessimism has its place,' she says.

So, when we think positively, are we just tricking ourselves that things will get better? It's a little more complicated than that, says Professor Fox. 'Where self-help books say "just think happy thoughts" it doesn't work.' But some degree of optimism can work to our advantage, because if we feel more positive, we will take more positive actions. 'Optimism gives you a sense of control,' she explains. So, to return to the example of the Olympics, if we had just repeated the mantra, 'the Olympics will be amazing, the Olympics will be amazing' it wouldn't have made it happen. In the event we actually did respond positively to them, but by taking the kind of actions – buying tickets to events, or getting involved as volunteers – that meant we ended up loving the whole experience.

More dramatically, positive thoughts can have concrete health benefits and can help us through certain situations, Professor Fox explains. In experiments on pain in which students are asked to keep their hands in a bucket of ice water for as long as they can stand it, students who believe they have been given a painkiller, but have in actual fact just been given a sugar pill, will keep their hand in longer than those who aren't given anything. Scans of their brains show they actually produce a surge of dopamine, a so-called 'happy' chemical, which combats the pain.

'Thomas Edison, the famous American inventor, said, "If I find 10,000 ways something won't work, I haven't failed. I am not discouraged, because every wrong attempt discarded is another step forward." In general, optimists will try harder and spend longer on something than pessimists,' says Professor Fox. 'They also believe they have some control over their life, and that's why they tend to be more successful.'

But don't shrug off your grumpy cynicism just yet. Professor Fox says a healthy dose of negativity can help us out, too. 'The amygdala – the fear system in our brain that helps us detect threat and danger – is really at the root of pessimism. Pessimism helps us suss out danger in our lives.' And although most of us are unlikely to need this reaction the same way our caveman ancestors did – for fight-or-flight reactions – fear is still a useful trait. 'A pessimistic outlook would work if you were setting up your own business,' says Professor Fox, 'to identify risk and avoid it.' So, there is a place for pessimism. 'They say the aeroplane was invented by an optimist and the parachute was invented by a pessimist. That's the reason I called the book *Rainy Brain, Sunny Brain*, because we need both.' Anticipate sunshine, but carry an umbrella and you should get along just fine.

31 The writer says that British attitudes to the 2012 Olympic Games

A illustrated an underlying mindset.
B contradicted stereotypes of national character.
C reflected a shift in public opinion.
D indicated the dangers of ambivalence.

32 In the second paragraph, we learn that Professor Fox believes being optimistic

A is more desirable than being pessimistic.
B is a necessary counter to our negativity.
C is likely to lead to unrealistic expectations.
D is as natural a quality as pessimism.

33 What does Professor Fox suggest about positive thinking in the third paragraph?

A It is difficult to find any sensible advice about it.
B It is ineffective unless carefully planned.
C It is desirable as it will lead to material benefits.
D It is likely to be the basis for practical achievement.

34 What is the writer illustrating by using the phrase 'the Olympics will be amazing'?

A the futility of merely thinking positively
B the way that positive thoughts can motivate people
C the importance of overcoming negative thinking
D the fact that people can be trained to think in certain ways

35 What point is exemplified by the reference to Thomas Edison?

A In order to be successful, we have to experience failure.
B Optimists gain success through persistence.
C Successful people are often unwilling to work for others.
D Success comes more easily to optimists than pessimists.

36 In the final paragraph, it is said that the invention of the parachute

A was a necessary consequence of the invention of the aeroplane.
B proved that humans always tend to fear the worst.
C was comparable to someone starting a company.
D demonstrated a readiness to confront the idea of risk.

Part 6

You are going to read an article about a tourist destination in Australia. Seven paragraphs have been removed from the extract. Choose from the paragraphs **A–H** the one which fits each gap (**37–43**). There is one extra paragraph which you do not need to use. Mark your answers **on the separate answer sheet.**

Visiting Uluru

One day in 1874, an explorer, Ernest Giles, struggled up a small hill and was confronted with a sight such as he could never have dreamed of finding. Before him, impossibly imposing, stood the most singular monolith on earth, the great red rock now known as Uluru. Hastening to report the find, he was informed that a man named William Gosse had chanced upon it a few days ahead of him and had already named it Ayers Rock after the South Australia governor.

37

So you are aware, as you drive to the park entrance, that you have driven 1,300 miles to look at something you have seen portrayed a thousand times already. In consequence, your mood as you approach this famous monolith is restrained, unexpectant – pessimistic even. And then you see it, and you are instantly transfixed. There, in the middle of a memorable and imposing emptiness, stands an eminence of exceptional nobility and grandeur, 1,150 feet high, a mile and a half long, five and a half miles around.

38

It's not that Uluru is bigger than you had supposed or more perfectly formed or in any way different from the impression you had created in your mind, but the very opposite. It is exactly what you expected it to be. You *know* this rock. You know it in a way that has nothing to do with calendars and the covers of souvenir books.

39

It is a motion much too faint to be understood or interpreted, but somehow you sense that this large, brooding, hypnotic presence has an importance to you at the species level – perhaps even at a sort of tadpole level – and that in some way your visit here is more than happenstance.

40

I'm suggesting nothing here, but I will say that if you were an intergalactic traveller who had broken down in our solar system, the obvious directions to rescuers would be: 'Go to the third planet and fly around till you see the big red rock. You can't miss it.' If ever on earth they dig up a 150,000-year-old rocket ship from the Galaxy Zog, this is where it will be. I'm not saying I expect it to happen; not saying that at all. I'm just observing that if I were looking for an ancient starship, this is where I would start digging.

41

You realize that you could spend quite a lot of time – possibly a worryingly large amount of time; possibly a sell-your-house-and-move-here-to-live-in-a-tent amount of time – just looking at the rock, gazing at it from many angles, never tiring of it. You can see yourself hanging out with much younger visitors and telling them: 'And the amazing thing is that every day it's different, you know what I'm saying? It's never the same rock twice. That's right, my friend – you put your finger on it there. It's awesome. It's an awesome thing.'

42

Instead, we stopped at the visitors' centre for a cup of coffee and to look at the displays, which were all to do with interpretations of the Dreamtime – the Aborigines' traditional conception of how the earth was formed and operates. There was nothing instructive in a historical or geological sense, which was disappointing because I was curious to know what Uluru is doing there. How do you get the biggest rock in existence onto the middle of an empty plain?

43

Afterwards we had one last drive around the rock before heading back to the lonely highway. We had been at the site for barely two hours, obviously not nearly enough time, but I realized as I turned around in my seat to watch it shrinking into the background behind us that there never could be enough, and I felt moderately comforted by that thought.

A It is less red than photographs have led you to expect but in every other way more arresting than you could ever have supposed. I have discussed this since with many other people, nearly all of whom agreed that they approached Uluru with a kind of fatigue, and were left amazed in a way they could not adequately explain.

B By the time you finally get there you are already a little sick of it. You can't go a day in Australia without seeing it four or five or six times – on postcards, on travel posters, on the cover of picture books – and as you get nearer, the frequency of exposure increases.

C Climbing up takes several hours and much exertion. Even when it's not too hot, lots of people get in trouble. Just the day before a Canadian had had to be rescued off a ledge from which he could not get either up or down. Fortunately, they close it to climbers when the weather is really warm, as it was this day.

D It is grounded in something much more elemental. In some odd way that you don't understand and can't begin to articulate you feel an acquaintance with it – a familiarity on an unfamiliar level. Somewhere in the deep sediment of your being some long-dormant fragment of memory has twitched or stirred.

E In fact, it is almost 300 miles across a largely featureless tract. Uluru's glory is that it stands alone in a boundless emptiness, but it does mean that you have to really want to see it; it's not something you're going to pass on the way to the beach.

F It turns out that Uluru is what is known as a bornhardt: a hunk of weather-resistant rock left standing when all else around it has worn away; but nowhere else on earth has one hunk of rock been left in such dramatic and solitary splendour or assumed such a pleasing smooth symmetry.

G I'm not saying that any of this is so. I'm just saying that this is how you feel. The other thought that strikes you – that struck me anyway – is that Uluru is not merely a splendid and mighty monolith, but also an extremely distinctive one.

H Quite apart from that initial shock of indefinable recognition, there is also the fact that Uluru is totally arresting. You cannot and don't want to stop looking at it. As you draw closer, it becomes even more interesting. It is less regular than you had imagined. There are more curves and more irregularities than are evident from even a couple of hundred yards away.

Part 7

You are going to read an article about the present-day importance of the moon landings. For questions **44–53**, choose from the sections (**A–E**). The sections may be chosen more than once. Mark your answers **on the separate answer sheet.**

In which section are the following mentioned?

a tribute to the ambitions of the space programme	**44**	
the accelerated development of technology	**45**	
a lack of encouragement to continue with a project	**46**	
various factors which made a task particularly challenging	**47**	
an individual example of the inspiring effects of Apollo	**48**	
an event marking the end of an era	**49**	
a spirited response to a seemingly impossible provocation	**50**	
the effects of the space programme on attitudes to sharing information	**51**	
a radical alteration of existing technology	**52**	
an influential combination of factors affecting the space programme	**53**	

Living in the Moon's Shadow

More than forty years on, why the moon landings are still having an impact today

A

On December 19, 1972, a sonic boom above the South Pacific signaled the completion of the Apollo program, as a tiny space capsule burst back through the blue sky. On board were the last three astronauts to visit the moon. The space race has changed the course of human history far more profoundly than anyone could have predicted in 1961, when a new president challenged America to land a man on the moon and return him safely to the Earth. No one present knew how to make it happen. But that wasn't going to stop them rising to President Kennedy's dare.

B

As progress in human space flight sped up through the 1960s, Ph.D. intake at American universities, particularly in the field of physics, increased almost threefold. Apollo was making America cleverer. Within weeks of Kennedy's speech, the Massachusetts Institute of Technology (MIT) was asked to work out the small matter of helping astronauts make a soft landing on a moving target hurtling through space 250,000 miles from Earth. To assist them in this, a small, lightweight computer was proposed by MIT. In the early '60s, computers often took up entire rooms. To miniaturize one enough to pack it into a modestly-sized craft they'd need new technology, so they turned to a brand new arrival on the technology scene: the integrated circuit.

C

Only a few companies were experimenting with these new micro-electronic components at the time; keen to help them perfect the performance of these novel miniature circuits, NASA ordered one million of them. The agency really only needed a few hundred, but, aware that they would be betting the lives of their astronauts on them, they were keen to make sure the manufacturers could make them as reliable as possible. Such a financial kickstart to a fledgling industry, coupled with another gift of Apollo — inspiration — would prove to be powerful drivers for technological change in the decades that followed. Those graduating across the world in the '70s and '80s had watched Apollo's engineers dream the impossible and then build it. As an act of human ingenuity, Apollo made them giddy, intoxicated on admiration and inspiration. As William Bainbridge put it in his book 'The Spaceflight Revolution', Apollo was 'a grand attempt to reach beyond the world of mundane life and transcend the ordinary limits of human existence through accomplishment of the miraculous – a story of engineers who tried to reach the heavens.'

D

Many of the people who have built the new tools of the Internet and the technological infrastructure that underpins it cite Apollo as their motivator. Professor Sir Martin Sweeting founded the world-renowned small satellite company SSTL, which revolutionized the industry. 'Apollo started me on this whole pathway of getting involved in space,' says Sweeting. 'The idea of being able to participate in something as exciting as a lunar landing, it stimulated an ambition, the dream of building my own satellite with my friends.' The idea of a small private enterprise launching a satellite was considered pretty crazy at the time, he points out. 'After building the first one, I had a lot of advice to go out and get a proper job. I'm sure that without Apollo I would have followed a more conventional career.'

E

Former NASA flight director Glynn Lunney witnessed the trickle-down straight from Apollo to the rest of us. 'We were asking people to do things 10 or 20 years ahead of when they would otherwise have done them. And they knew it. They stepped up to it and succeeded. Today's cell phones, wireless equipment, tablet computers and so on are a result of the fact that the country did this high-tech thing and made this large portfolio of technologies available.' Today's population, over half of whom weren't born when those last astronauts returned from the moon, use these inventions to communicate with each other freely and without a thought for geographical and cultural differences. The gifts of Apollo continue to ripple down the decades, and still have the power to unite and inspire us.

WRITING (1 hour 30 minutes)

Part 1

Read the two texts below.

Write an essay summarising and evaluating the key points from both texts. Use your own words throughout as far as possible, and include your own ideas in your answers.

Write your answer in **240–280** words.

1

Being at home

For some people, it is only at home that they can truly relax. It is the place they go to to recover from both the excitements and the stress of their everyday life: the noisy hubbub of the city, the pressures of study and work, and the busy commute through rush-hour traffic. They appreciate the opportunity to reflect on all that has happened that day. They can contemplate the day's significant events either in the peace and quiet of their own room or through participating in a discussion over a meal.

Home and away

For many of us, life at home can be rather restrictive, or simply dull, so we escape to public places where we can socialise and be ourselves, such as cafés and coffee bars. Yet home is still a place where people can express their personalities. The choice of furniture, the colour scheme, and the paintings or posters displayed on the walls, will all say a great deal about the person who lives there. Visiting a friend's home for the first time may well reveal aspects of their personality which were previously unknown to us.

Write your **essay**.

Part 2

Write an answer to **one** of the questions **2–5** in this part. Write your answer in **280–320** words in an appropriate style.

---

2 You have recently worked as a volunteer, coaching teenagers at a sports camp designed to encourage young people to take up new sports. The organisers have asked you to write a report for the website. You should briefly describe your responsibilities as a coach for two different sports. You should also evaluate how valuable the sports camp was for the teenagers overall and recommend how it could be improved in future.

Write your **report**.

3 You have recently read some letters in a magazine discussing the question 'What are good manners?'. The magazine has invited readers to join the debate. You decide to write a letter in which you briefly describe one or two examples of what you consider to be good manners, explaining why behaving politely in those particular situations is necessary. You should also evaluate just how important good manners are nowadays.

Write your **letter**.

4 A film magazine has invited readers to submit reviews of films which are set in the future, but deal with themes relevant to today's world, such as our relationship with technology or environmental problems. You decide to submit a review briefly describing such a film and explaining why its themes are relevant today. You should also consider how important it is for films set in the future to say something about contemporary society.

Write your **review**.

5 Write an answer to **one** of the following two questions based on **one** of the titles below. Write **5(a)** or **5(b)** at the beginning of your answer.

(a) Tracy Chevalier: *Girl with a Pearl Earring*
'The earring would complete the painting. It would also put me on the street.'
Your class tutor has asked you to write an essay assessing the significance of the pearl earrings in Griet's story, and explaining the way in which the earrings contribute to her losing her position in the Vermeer household.

Write your **essay**.

(b) Tobias Hill: *The Cryptographer*
An English language magazine is running a series of articles dealing with the theme of money, and has asked its readers to send in articles for the series. You decide to write an article considering the importance of money in the relationship between John Law and Anna Moore in *The Cryptographer*. You should also explain why you think an article about this novel would be worth including in the series.

Write your **article**.

LISTENING (40 minutes approximately)

Part 1

You will hear three different extracts. For questions **1–6**, choose the answer (**A**, **B** or **C**) which fits best according to what you hear.

There are two questions for each extract.

Extract One

You hear a well-known scientist giving a talk to a group of science graduates at their graduation ceremony.

1 Why does he mention the field of climate science?

A to emphasise the importance of examining data carefully
B to warn about the dangers of ignoring the evidence
C to suggest that some subjects are more controversial than others

2 What is the aim of his talk?

A to point out the value of sharing scientific knowledge
B to highlight what is most relevant in scientific study
C to criticise the way much scientific data is reported

Extract Two

You hear part of an interview with a psychologist on the subject of memory.

3 What is the psychologist's attitude to people who cannot forget?

A He criticises their limitations.
B He understands their uncertainty.
C He envies their ability.

4 The psychologist contrasts human memory and computer memory in order to

A demonstrate the versatility of human memory.
B emphasise the capacity of computer memory.
C question the provisional nature of perception.

Extract Three

You hear two media studies lecturers comparing electronic readers and printed materials.

5 Which aspect of printed books do they agree about?

A their practical inconvenience
B their physical appeal
C their environmental cost

6 What is the man doing when he refers to newspapers?

A deliberating on their future
B defending their role
C predicting their disappearance

Part 2

You will hear a student called Tom giving a presentation about non-native species of animals in Australia, and the problems they cause.

For questions **7–15**, complete the sentences with a word or short phrase.

Rabbits introduced from Europe are widespread in Australia except in regions where **(7)** .... is present.

According to Tom, rabbits' feeding habits mean that foods such as **(8)** .... are unavailable for native Australian birds.

An introduced species known as the cane toad can kill **(9)** .... as well as smaller creatures with its poison.

Camels were introduced to Australia to carry supplies to **(10)** .... in remote desert areas.

Australian camels particularly enjoy eating the **(11)** .... of the apricot tree.

When water is scarce, camels may destroy village **(12)** .... in poor communities.

It is too expensive to use **(13)** .... as a widespread means of controlling invasive species.

Successful control measures have been implemented on one **(14)** .... but other places are more difficult.

In Australia, **(15)** .... is in place to prevent the problem from getting worse.

Part 3

You will hear part of an interview with two British architects, Malcolm Fletcher and Alison Brooks, about the design of new low-cost housing.

For questions **16–20**, choose the answer (**A, B, C** or **D**) which fits best according to what you hear.

---

16 What view is expressed about the government's plans to build houses on greenfield sites?

A Opposition groups are unlikely to have any real influence.
B It may be possible to create space by demolishing some existing buildings.
C There is a more important priority than preserving the countryside.
D New developments should show continuity with what has gone before.

17 What does Malcolm regard as special about the Newhall housing development in Essex?

A the involvement of local people in the planning process
B the unusual attitude of the original landowners
C the good relationship between the builders and the architect
D the freedom given to the designers

18 The aspect of Margaret Gibbs's houses which both Alison and Malcolm appreciate is

A their visual appeal.
B their generous dimensions.
C their structural strength.
D their internal layout.

19 When designing the space around the Essex houses, Margaret Gibbs

A attempted to integrate homes with recreational areas.
B conceded to the general demand for a garden.
C allowed a bigger external area than usual.
D aimed to safeguard the inhabitants' privacy.

20 What do Malcolm and Alison agree about the aesthetic qualities of buildings?

A Architectural form may sometimes take precedence over function.
B Beauty is an intrinsic aspect of good architecture.
C There is little consensus concerning what constitutes good style.
D Popular notions of good taste inevitably change over time.

Part 4

You will hear five short extracts in which people talk about academic conferences they have attended.

TASK ONE

For questions **21–25**, choose from the list (**A–H**) the reason each speaker gives for wanting to attend an academic conference.

TASK TWO

For questions **26–30**, choose from the list (**A–H**) how each speaker felt about the first presenter.

While you listen, you must complete both tasks.

A to learn about new trends

B to listen to a celebrated speaker

C to gain inspiration

D to re-connect with old friends

E to discuss shared problems

F to present a paper

G to enjoy a perk

H to meet publishers

Speaker 1		21
Speaker 2		22
Speaker 3		23
Speaker 4		24
Speaker 5		25

A disappointed by his lack of substance

B impressed by his claims

C sceptical about his research results

D amused by his anecdotes

E embarrassed by his hesitations

F bored by his repetitions

G concerned by his inaccurracy

H annoyed by his original ideas

Speaker 1		26
Speaker 2		27
Speaker 3		28
Speaker 4		29
Speaker 5		30

SPEAKING (16 minutes)

There are two examiners. One (the interlocutor) conducts the test, providing you with the necessary materials and explaining what you have to do. The other examiner (the assessor) will be introduced to you, but then takes no further part in the interaction.

Part 1 (2 minutes)

The interlocutor first asks you and your partner a few questions which focus on information about yourselves.

Part 2 (4 minutes)

In this part of the test you and your partner are asked to talk together. The interlocutor places a set of pictures on the table in front of you. There may be only one picture in the set or as many as seven pictures. This stimulus provides the basis for a discussion. The interlocutor first asks an introductory question which focuses on two of the pictures (or in the case of a single picture, on aspects of the picture). After about a minute, the interlocutor gives you both a decision-making task based on the same set of pictures.

The pictures for Part 2 are on page C3 of the colour section.

Part 3 (10 minutes)

You are each given the opportunity to talk for two minutes, to comment after your partner has spoken and to take part in a more general discussion.

The interlocutor gives you a card with a question written on it and asks you to talk about it for two minutes. After you have spoken, the interlocutor asks you both another question related to the topic on the card, addressing your partner first. This procedure is repeated, so that your partner receives a card and speaks for two minutes and a follow-up question is asked.

Finally, the interlocutor asks some further questions, which lead to a discussion on a general theme related to the subjects already covered in Part 3.

The cards for Part 3 are on pages C6–C7 of the colour section.

Test 3

READING AND USE OF ENGLISH (1 hour 30 minutes)

Part 1

For questions **1–8**, read the text below and decide which answer (**A**, **B**, **C** or **D**) best fits each gap.

Mark your answers **on the separate answer sheet**.

There is an example at the beginning (**0**).

0 **A** despatched **B** launched **C** commenced **D** embarked

0	A	B	C	D
	▭	▬	▭	▭

A Cosmic Directory

Scientists at Puerto Rico University in Arecibo have recently **(0)** .... a cosmic directory that lists the planets and moons most likely to **(1)** .... alien life. They created the catalogue to make sense of the ever-increasing number of distant worlds that are visible with modern telescopes. They believe it will help astronomers, and others with an interest, to compare faraway worlds and keep **(2)** .... on the most habitable ones as researchers discover them.

The catalogue ranks the habitability of planets and moons according to three **(3)** ....: their surface temperature, their similarity to Earth and their capacity to **(4)** .... organisms that **(5)** .... at the bottom of the food chain. It suggests that among hundreds of candidates, only a few planets are **(6)** .... habitable, and gives high **(7)** .... for habitability to even fewer. The database also holds information on the **(8)** .... of the planets, their probable mass and the type and age of the stars they orbit.

1	**A** shield	**B** protect	**C** harbour	**D** safeguard
2	**A** eyes	**B** logs	**C** tabs	**D** check
3	**A** principles	**B** criteria	**C** concepts	**D** scales
4	**A** uphold	**B** maintain	**C** preserve	**D** sustain
5	**A** lurk	**B** loiter	**C** hide	**D** hover
6	**A** potentially	**B** plausibly	**C** predictably	**D** prospectively
7	**A** levels	**B** notes	**C** totals	**D** scores
8	**A** situation	**B** destination	**C** location	**D** orientation

Part 2

For questions **9–16**, read the text below and think of the word which best fits each space. Use only **one** word in each space. There is an example at the beginning **(0)**. Write your answers **IN CAPITAL LETTERS on the separate answer sheet**

Example: | **0** | W | I | T | H | O | U | T |

Translation

In today's globalised world, the role the translator plays is, **(0)** .... a doubt, crucial. Each and **(9)** .... time translators set to work they have a heavy responsibility to communicate as accurately as possible. A poor translation might merely cause amusement, but at **(10)** ...., the consequences could sometimes be extremely serious.

There are a great many problems encountered in the translation process, some deriving **(11)** .... the grammatical differences between languages and others caused by idioms, not to mention highly specific cultural references that some argue, with good **(12)** .... perhaps, cannot be successfully translated.

It **(13)** .... without saying that translators should have a well-developed sensitivity to their mother tongue and the second language they work with. But whereas once they needed little **(14)** .... than exceptional linguistic skills, translators nowadays may require specialist knowledge of areas such as medicine, law or technology.

One factor they consider is how the translation sounds. Here, they may make **(15)** .... of strategies such as reading their translation aloud, thereby ensuring that words are not put in a sentence if, **(16)** .... individually accurate and appropriate, together they sound harsh or unpleasant.

Part 3

For questions **17–24**, read the text below. Use the word given in capitals at the end of some of the lines to form a word that fits in the space in the same line. There is an example at the beginning (**0**). Write your answers **IN CAPITAL LETTERS on the separate answer sheet**.

Example: | 0 | O | C | C | A | S | I | O | N | A | L | L | Y | | | | | | | |

The need to read

All children **(0)** .... ask why we should bother reading. Now, 500 years after	**OCCASION**
Gutenberg's printing press **(17)** .... reading, recent technological advances	**DEMOCRACY**
mean psychologists may be able to find an answer. Using brain scans, they	
have found we create mental simulations of situations **(18)** .... in a book and	**COUNTER**
weave these together with real-life experiences to create a new way of thinking.	
This is something many of us will understand **(19)** .... when we look back	**INSTINCT**
and realise that an **(20)** .... book that we read in the past had an absolutely	**STAND**
(21) .... effect on how we view the world. This transformation takes place	**REVOLVE**
only when we lose ourselves **(22)** .... in a book. Studies have found this deep	**CONDITION**
reading makes us more sympathetic, more alert to the **(23)** .... lives of others.	**IN**
Here then is the irrefutable answer to our initial question, and it means that reading	
must continue to be **(24)** .... in our culture.	**BED**

Part 4

For questions **25–30**, complete the second sentence so that it has a similar meaning to the first sentence, using the word given. **Do not change the word given**. You must use between **three** and **eight** words, including the word given. Here is an example (**0**).

Example:

0 Do you mind if I watch you while you paint?

objection

Do you .... you while you paint?

0	*have any objection to my watching*

Write **only** the missing words **on the separate answer sheet**.

---

25 I don't think you'll find that many road atlases have such detailed maps.

few

I .... have such detailed maps.

26 The owner of the shop said that we didn't have to buy anything; we could just look round.

obligation

The owner of the shop said that we .... a purchase; we could just look round.

27 Martin was too lazy to present any of his ideas at the meeting yesterday.

bothered

Martin .... forward any of his ideas at the meeting yesterday.

28 Once he'd handed in his entry, the only thing Tom could do was wait for the judge's decision.

nothing

Once he'd handed in his entry, there .... wait for the judge's decision.

29 Philip said that his friends were surprised when he suddenly decided to retire.

came

Philip said that his .... to his friends.

30 Susan doesn't intend to climb that mountain again.

has

Susan .... that mountain again.

Part 5

You are going to read an article about the 19th century French painter, Edouard Manet. For questions **31–36**, choose the answer (**A**, **B**, **C** or **D**) which you think fits best according to the text. Mark your answers **on the separate answer sheet.**

Manet: Portraying Life

A new exhibition of portraits by the great French painter, Manet

It is probably fair to say that Manet is not associated with the idea of penetrating portraiture. Although he used models as well as friends and insisted on painting only from prolonged, frequent sittings, it wasn't to dig deep into the psyche of his subjects, but to comment on their place through their appearance. All Manet's works were an assault. All, except for the flower paintings so derided by modern curators, were efforts to catch something of the contemporary world about him.

Very few of Manet's extensive output of portraits were commissioned. As the son of wealthy parents, he didn't need to earn his crust this way. Instead he painted his family, particularly his wife, the Dutch-born Suzanne Leenhoff, and her son, Léon, friends from among his wide circle of cultural contacts and professional models. What was it that he was seeking from these pictures? The simplest answer is 'realism', the observation of what was new and contemporary, which his mentor, the poet and critic Charles Baudelaire, proclaimed as the true test of modern art. Realism meant not just painting accurately from life, but stripping art of all the connotations of moral lesson and monumentality found in traditional art. Its heroes would become the man about town, the observer, the dandy.

But realism in portraiture for Manet was never merely a matter of recording the face and figure with verisimilitude. 'I cannot do anything without the model,' declared Manet. 'I do not know how to invent .... If I amount to anything today, I put it down to precise interpretation and faithful analysis.' But it was the 'interpretation' and 'analysis' that made him so different. With men it was to convey what they meant for the world about them. His portrait of Zacharie Astruc, the writer and critic who had done much to support him in his early years, is divided into two parts. On the right, Astruc sits somewhat pompously, his hand thrust into his jacket, while to the left is seen his wife in the kitchen, along with the symbols of the domestic life which underpins him. The portrait of Emile Zola, another great supporter, arranges the novelist with the attributes of his art criticism, an open book on Spanish art in his hand and a Japanese print above his desk.

With women it is quite different. Manet was clearly entranced by them, soaking up their vivacity, admiring their poise and revelling in a pretty face. It doesn't appear to have been predatory. Indeed the most touching pictures in the exhibition remain those of his wife, whom he painted more often and for longer than any other sitter; she is depicted at the piano, stroking the cat, resting in the conservatory. The plump and humorous face is always done with fondness, the background painted with quick, fleeting brushstrokes that envelop the sitter in the flowers around her or the dress she is wearing.

For Manet, dress was an assertion of modernity, a way of depicting the modern bourgeois woman who was emerging from the constraints of an aristocratic past. But, going round these galleries, it is difficult not to believe that he thought women the better, or at least the more life-enhancing, of the species. It is noticeable that in almost all the portraits of couples or couples with children – in the rather touching portrait of *The Monet Family in Their Garden at Argenteuil* and *In the Garden* of 1870 – it is the women who take the foremost role. It's more than their attractions and the dress; it's that Manet looks on them as the future more than the men in the background.

In Manet's portraiture, the parts don't add up to a whole. His efforts to start each picture anew don't make for an easy synthesis and, as such, gallery curators struggle to categorise them. A gathering of these varied and sometimes uneven works can't express all of the man. For that you really do need his bigger set pieces. This exhibition is not a gathering of masterpieces. Nor is it a comprehensive showing of his portraiture, given the paucity of the borrowings from France. But what you have is the outpouring of one of the towering geniuses of art who stood each time before his canvas with a subject, thought and thought about what he wanted to say and then worked to express it. Forget the whole, just look at the individual works and feel the mind behind them.

31 How does the writer say Manet's portraiture differed from that found in traditional art?

A It was less commercial in style.
B It demonstrated superior technical ability.
C It was non-judgemental in approach.
D It showed the influence of a literary movement.

32 According to the writer, Manet believed he was successful because he

A had worked with the right people.
B tried to convey his ideas accurately.
C could see his subjects as they saw themselves.
D was capable of highly life-like portraits.

33 References to the portraits of Astruc and Zola suggest Manet's

A disdain for self-important men.
B belief in the importance of context.
C idea that nobody is beyond criticism.
D view that all men are basically the same.

34 What do Manet's paintings of his wife show the viewer?

A the way he felt about women in general
B the important role his wife played in furthering his career
C the variety of locations in which he enjoyed painting
D the ability he had to capture the appearance of a sitter

35 Why does the writer think that Manet's portraits are problematic for gallery curators?

A There is no common element running through them.
B They are not sufficiently consistent in style.
C They do not represent the true man behind them.
D There are no truly outstanding pieces among them.

36 What does the writer conclude about the exhibition?

A It tells us more about Manet than is obvious at first sight.
B It gives an insight into the total commitment of a great painter.
C It provides some serious challenges for the viewer.
D It proves that art cannot be appreciated without understanding the artist.

Part 6

You are going to read an extract from a book about a trip to the country of Malawi. Seven paragraphs have been removed from the extract. Choose from the paragraphs **A–H** the one which fits each gap (**37–43**). There is one extra paragraph which you do not need to use. Mark your answers **on the separate answer sheet.**

Lake Malawi's lost resort

Novelist ***Marina Lewycka*** *reveals how getting lost in the African bush led her to find paradise by Lake Malawi*

It's easy to get off the beaten track in Malawi. In fact it can be difficult to stay on it, as we found three years ago when we were driving up the lake road from Salima towards Nkhata Bay for a week's holiday, in my daughter's old low-slung Nissan Bluebird, her boyfriend at the wheel.

37 ______

It became obvious that we weren't going to get to Nkhata Bay, and we'd have to stop somewhere overnight. We drove to a couple of upmarket lodges, but they were closed, or full, or just didn't like the look of us. We were directed to other, more remote places, which either didn't exist, or were also full; we were beginning to get worried.

38 ______

After a kilometre or so, it divided into a number of less distinct ones. They were definitely not beaten – they were hardly more than faint trails. There was no light ahead – in fact, there was no light anywhere, apart from the stars, which hung so close and bright you almost felt you could reach up and pick them out of the sky like low-hanging fruit.

39 ______

Beyond the narrow beam of our headlights, it was pitch black. All around us were prickly bushes, their vague menacing shapes blocking out the lie of the land. Swarms of mosquitoes smelled our fear, and swooped.

40 ______

Then we heard voices, coming from somewhere beyond the bushes. Two boys appeared, followed by an older man. They greeted us, grinning. In fact, they might have been laughing at us. We didn't care. Greetings were exchanged. People are very polite in Malawi.

41 ______

We left the car on and followed them down a series of dark winding tracks, without knowing who they were or where they were taking us. At last we came to a small hamlet, half a dozen thatched mud-walled houses, all closed up for the night. They called, and a man emerged from one of the houses; he was tall, and blind in one eye. We asked whether we could stay at the Maia Beach accommodation. Apparently unsurprised by these three pale strangers who'd turned up on his doorstep in the middle of the night, he smiled his assent. He fetched keys, and we followed him as he set off again down a winding track through the bushes.

42 ______

And there, along the shore, was a cluster of small bamboo huts. One was opened up for us. A torch was found. A price was agreed. Bedding was brought. The mosquito nets were full of holes, but I had a sewing kit, and the kindness of our hosts more than made up for any discomforts.

43 ______

The next morning we were woken by bright sunlight, needling through the cracks in the bamboo wall, and the sound of children's voices. I pushed open the door of our hut, and gasped at the sheer beauty of our surroundings. We'd landed in paradise. There, just a few metres away, was a crescent of silver sand lapped by the crystal water of the lake. A couple of palm trees waved lazy branches against the sun. A gaggle of ragged smiling children had gathered at our door, chattering excitedly. As I stepped outside, they fell silent for a moment, then burst into a chorus: 'Good afternoon. Good morning. How are you? Do you speak English? What is your name?'

A It didn't take many words to explain what had happened. With some careful manoeuvering and some brute force, slowly, slowly, we inched on to firmer ground. We asked for directions to the Maia Beach resort. It transpired that it had closed down last year but someone in a nearby village had a key.

B It was that dangerous time when the roads are swarming with villagers and their animals, and drivers of vehicles without functioning lights or brakes career around potholes, also hurrying homewards. For twilight is short in Malawi, and when night comes, the darkness is absolute.

C After a while they thinned out and I could see the soft star-lit glimmer of Lake Malawi spread before us like a wide swathe of grey silk, so still you'd never have guessed it was water, apart from a faint ripple that wrinkled its surface when the breeze stirred.

D We drove back slowly, seeking a turning off the road, a track towards the lake, but there was no opening, not even a gap between the prickly bushes where the track should have been, only the same unremitting vista of low trees, bushes and sand.

E This place, we were told, had been created by an English couple who intended to use the proceeds to fund a school and a health centre in the village. But few tourists had ever made it here, and no one knew whether the couple would ever return.

F Suddenly, out of the dusk, a crooked, hand-painted wooden sign flickered across our headlights: 'Maia Beach Cafe Accommodation'. We let out a cheer, executed a U-turn, and set out down the sandy track signposted towards the beach.

G We held our breath and listened to the silence. Somewhere far away there was a sound of drumming, and we could smell wood smoke, which suggested some kind of habitation.

H Then, all of a sudden, our wheels hit a patch of soft sand, skidded, and sank in. Getting out to assess the situation, we saw that three wheels were hopelessly churning up the sand; the fourth was spinning free, perched over a sandy bluff with a four-foot drop beneath. If we slipped down there, we would never, ever get the car out again.

Part 7

You are going to read extracts from an article about favourite old songs. For questions **44–53**, choose from the sections (**A–E**). The extracts may be chosen more than once. Mark your answers **on the separate answer sheet.**

Which extract mentions

the possibility of varying interpretations of this version of the song?	**44**	
the technical limitations of the musician?	**45**	
an example of the artist adopting a particular identity?	**46**	
awareness of self-delusion?	**47**	
a restored reputation?	**48**	
the increased personal significance that a song has come to have?	**49**	
some thoughts on the nature of hero worship?	**50**	
a suggestion that all is not lost?	**51**	
the ability of music to evoke the past?	**52**	
an instance of personal satisfaction?	**53**	

Old Music

Five people write about musicians and songs that have been important to them in their life

A

***At Last I Am Free* by Robert Wyatt**

Originally written for those masters of disco, Chic, it seems a long journey to Robert Wyatt's version. Wyatt is one of the great heroes of British counter-culture, whose blend of political commitment and musical experiment has led to a career of almost unrivalled range and influence. On this song he combines the heartbreaking honesty familiar from his other work with a voice that is somehow at once shrill but deeply soulful and communicative. The lyrics speak of a failing relationship but the way Wyatt sings it could be about anything – any momentous parting or new beginnings. The line 'I can hardly see in front of me' is one of those phrases in pop music that come along from time to time that mean almost nothing yet bulge under the weight of a thousand projected meanings for a thousand different listeners.

B

***Another Day* by Roy Harper**

Decades on from its 1974 release 'Another Day' still strikes me as one of the most poignant and beautiful songs ever; a regretful ode to a lost love encountered once again, full of thwarted possibilities that the singer acknowledges but refuses to grasp and with regrets on both sides about things that should have been said but were not. At the song's end, even the possibility for words runs out as the former lovers stand with the shades of their former selves awkwardly between them. Others have covered the song, but none is better than Harper's original version, which Harper himself believes to be one of the 'best love songs I wrote'. Although Harper's beautiful, angry and sometimes passionate songs fell into a quiet obscurity for a while, these days he is namechecked at almost every turn by modern-day artists.

C

***Say Hello Wave Goodbye* by Soft Cell**

This song is a time machine for men and women of a certain age. Soft Cell had questionable credibility even then, so this was always a guilty pleasure for me. It has one of the best opening lines, ever – 'I never went to the Pink Flamingo, but if I had, I am sure I would have found someone in the doorway, crying in the rain'. It was all slightly seedy – a down-at-heel, defeated romanticism. The oboe hitting the high notes offers a sharp reminder that singer Marc Almond can't manage the same, but the combination of the two works a treat, backed by a rhythm that doesn't seem to want to end. Back then, the pain was all imagined. Thirty years on, you can wallow in proper melancholy all you like. But make sure the kids are out.

D

***Maggie May* by Rod Stewart**

I once went to an 18th birthday party disco. 'Maggie May' came on and instantly the place erupted; at least half a dozen strapping blokes more suited to the great outdoors started marching around clutching invisible microphone stands. It was a bizarre sight, but testimony to the hold that Stewart had at that time over lads who felt compelled to ape him. What is it about that song? A mood of end-of-summer rueful regret, mingled with rite of passage reminiscence? It came out in September 1971; I had just broken up with a girl who was admittedly nothing like woman-of-the-world Maggie. But 'you made a first-class fool out of me' – well, I kidded myself that rang true, at the time. Perhaps it was just the footballs, scarves, and glorious, ramshackle live appearances that appealed to men my age.

E

***Martha* by Tom Waits**

Written when Tom Waits was just 24, 'Martha' finds this earliest incarnation of one of the US's most intriguing musical characters dropping comfortably into the slippers of a much, much older man. Calling long-distance to an old flame, he lays his heart bare about their past together and offers the beautifully underplayed revelation that he is still in love with her. The poignancy of this call taking place when both are probably now well into their 50s is given added weight – that so much time could never erase this strength of feeling. The lyrics make you wish you could be there to see these two fictional characters reunited. In the age of social media, this track stands as a memorial to a time when you could easily lose touch with someone so very close to you, as time marched brutally on.

WRITING (1 hour 30 minutes)

Part 1

Read the two texts below.

Write an essay summarising and evaluating the key points from both texts. Use your own words throughout as far as possible, and include your own ideas in your answers.

Write your answer in **240–280** words.

1

Dress and Image

When professionals such as bank managers or lawyers wear formal clothes, they are often sending out a clear signal that they wish to maintain a degree of distance and detachment from those they serve. Their style of dress suggests that the atmosphere is unlikely to be light-hearted or relaxed. In fact, there is no doubt that many of us would be somewhat uncomfortable if we walked into the office of a bank manager or lawyer who was dressed casually. Somehow, formal clothes communicate the message 'I am competent and you can trust me', and naturally we feel reassured by this.

The Impact of Dress

Many jobs involve wearing a uniform but the authority this suggests can be intimidating to some people who may instinctively feel that they are put at a disadvantage. For some purposes therefore, such as when police have to deal with particularly vulnerable people, informal clothes may be more appropriate. Of course, there are some important public occasions, such as coronations and state funerals, for which the wearing of elaborate formal dress is an integral part of the ceremony; it might be deemed disrespectful if this critical custom were not observed.

Write your **essay**.

Part 2

Write an answer to **one** of the questions **2–5** in this part. Write your answer in **280–320** words in an appropriate style.

---

2 An English language magazine is running a series on the topic of happiness. You decide to send in an article. You should briefly describe one or two situations in which you have experienced a sense of happiness. You should also analyse what contributes to feelings of happiness for many people, and suggest whether the pursuit of happiness is a worthwhile aim.

Write your **article**.

3 A cultural magazine is planning a series on historical exhibitions organised by museums that have captured the imagination of the public. You decide to submit a review of an exhibition with a historical theme that has impressed you. Your review should briefly describe the exhibition, explain why you think it was successful, and assess the importance of such exhibitions in educating the public about history.

Write your **review**.

4 An international newspaper is inviting readers to contribute letters on the topic of speakers who have inspired them. You decide to write a letter about a speaker you heard recently. You should explain what was particularly inspiring about this speaker and assess the value of listening to inspirational speakers in general.

Write your **letter**.

5 Write an answer to **one** of the following two questions based on **one** of the titles below. Write **5(a)** or **5(b)** at the beginning of your answer.

(a) Chinua Achebe: *Things Fall Apart*
Members of your reading group have been asked to review books which deal with the theme of justice in different societies. You decide to write a review of *Things Fall Apart.* Your review should briefly consider the approach to justice taken by Okonkwo's clan and assess the impact that approach has on people's lives.

Write your **review**.

(b) J.B. Priestley: *An Inspector Calls*
As a member of your college drama group you have been asked to write a report for the group in preparation for their production of *An Inspector Calls*. Your report should briefly describe the ways in which the Birling family respond to the Inspector's questions, and how the attitudes of Mr. and Mrs. Birling contrast with those of their children.

Write your **report**.

LISTENING (40 minutes approximately)

Part 1

You will hear three different extracts.

For questions **1–6**, choose the answer (**A**, **B** or **C**) which fits best according to what you hear.

There are two questions for each extract.

Extract One

You hear a woman talking on the radio about a small mammal called the hedgehog.

1 What is her attitude to the reduction in the number of hedgehogs in Britain?

A She is concerned at the part played by cats.
B She is disinclined to take it very seriously.
C She thinks it may affect other animals.

2 What does she suggest about threats to wildlife?

A Some species are more important than others.
B Politicians are too slow in taking action.
C There are more pressing priorities.

Extract Two

You hear an entrepreneur called Patrick Schwerdtfeger giving a talk at a business conference.

3 Patrick uses the example of a skyscraper

A to emphasise how competitive people need to be.
B to illustrate that anything is possible with determination.
C to show that you need imagination to succeed.

4 Patrick thinks that 'realistic' goals

A display a lack of ambition.
B may offer little sense of achievement.
C can be too popular.

Extract Three

You hear part of an interview with a man called Maurice Parks, who owns a small independent publishing company.

5 Maurice feels his professional approach is unusual because

A he does not make assumptions about authors.
B he is more selective than traditional publishers.
C he does not believe in rushing the editing process.

6 Maurice says editors in big publishing companies are driven by

A the search for new formats.
B the need to create profits.
C the safeguarding of their reputation.

Part 2

You will hear a radio presenter called Tom Lee describing the psychological effects of the colour red on humans and animals.

For questions **7–15**, complete the sentences with a word or short phrase.

Psychologists at a British university found those taking part in **(7)** .... competitions got more points when they wore red.

Tom says it is becoming increasingly clear that colours affect how the human **(8)** .... behaves.

Anthropologist Ella Beecham identified a possible **(9)** .... when she discovered how colours were assigned in some Olympic events.

Beecham found wearing red affected results most when wrestlers were what is referred to as **(10)** ....

Beecham believes that unexpected results may occur when a **(11)** .... has an unconscious preference for red.

Beecham investigated whether different levels of **(12)** .... had a favourable effect on those playing in the same team.

Tom uses the words **(13)** .... and .... to describe the meaning that red often has in nature.

Fish in an aquarium behaved in a way normally reserved for encounters with **(14)** .... when a red vehicle was nearby.

In mandrill monkeys, red signifies the **(15)** .... of the male in cases of possible conflict.

Part 3

You will hear a radio programme in which two people, Alison Kreel and David Walsh, who each run a food business, are discussing the premises they share.

For questions **16–20**, choose the answer (**A**, **B**, **C** or **D**) which fits best according to what you hear.

---

16 Alison and David agree that the market for quality food products

- **A** is experiencing greater growth than ever.
- **B** is becoming increasingly sophisticated.
- **C** has a thirst for constant innovation.
- **D** can only thrive in particular locations.

17 David thinks that the Siston building attracted funding easily because

- **A** it was considered the best way to start regenerating a run-down industrial area.
- **B** it was less risky than financing individual entrepreneurs.
- **C** it was thought it would give new food companies valuable support.
- **D** it was part of a drive to increase local employment opportunities.

18 They both agree the main benefit of using a shared kitchen space is cost savings and

- **A** being able to get advice from fellow entrepreneurs.
- **B** being able to share marketing opportunities.
- **C** having a supportive working environment.
- **D** having access to top-of-the-range equipment and facilities.

19 How has Alison's vision for her business changed since moving into the Siston building?

- **A** She has realised that she needs to expand her range of products.
- **B** She now sees that opening a shop and café would have been too risky.
- **C** She has decided she prefers the idea of selling to small local businesses.
- **D** She no longer thinks becoming a nationally recognised brand is achievable.

20 What advice would Alison and David give to any aspiring entrepreneur?

- **A** Work out costs carefully.
- **B** Don't spend too much time planning.
- **C** Get some relevant work experience.
- **D** Don't waste time on low margin products.

Part 4

You will hear five short extracts in which people talk about studying abroad.

TASK ONE

For questions **21–25**, choose from the list (**A–H**) the reason each speaker gives for wanting to study abroad.

TASK TWO

For questions **26–30**, choose from the list (**A–H**) how each speaker felt about their studies abroad.

While you listen, you must complete both tasks.

Task One

A to experience another culture
B to improve foreign language competence
C to improve job prospects
D to get a different perspective on a subject
E to experience a different teaching method
F to make useful contacts
G to become more independent
H to live closer to extended family

Speaker 1 [ ] **21**
Speaker 2 [ ] **22**
Speaker 3 [ ] **23**
Speaker 4 [ ] **24**
Speaker 5 [ ] **25**

Task Two

A reassured by the available support facilities
B concerned about the high tuition fees
C impressed with the international nature of the institution
D surprised by the contrast with undergraduate study
E disappointed by the academic standards
F satisfied with the accommodation
G pleased to find the learning goals achievable
H challenged by the amount of self study

Speaker 1 [ ] **26**
Speaker 2 [ ] **27**
Speaker 3 [ ] **28**
Speaker 4 [ ] **29**
Speaker 5 [ ] **30**

SPEAKING (16 minutes)

There are two examiners. One (the interlocutor) conducts the test, providing you with the necessary materials and explaining what you have to do. The other examiner (the assessor) will be introduced to you, but then takes no further part in the interaction.

Part 1 (2 minutes)

The interlocutor first asks you and your partner a few questions which focus on information about yourselves.

Part 2 (4 minutes)

In this part of the test you and your partner are asked to talk together. The interlocutor places a set of pictures on the table in front of you. There may be only one picture in the set or as many as seven pictures. This stimulus provides the basis for a discussion. The interlocutor first asks an introductory question which focuses on two of the pictures (or in the case of a single picture, on aspects of the picture). After about a minute, the interlocutor gives you both a decision-making task based on the same set of pictures.

The pictures for Part 2 are on page C4 of the colour section.

Part 3 (10 minutes)

You are each given the opportunity to talk for two minutes, to comment after your partner has spoken and to take part in a more general discussion.

The interlocutor gives you a card with a question written on it and asks you to talk about it for two minutes. After you have spoken, the interlocutor asks you both another question related to the topic on the card, addressing your partner first. This procedure is repeated, so that your partner receives a card and speaks for two minutes and a follow-up question is asked.

Finally, the interlocutor asks some further questions, which lead to a discussion on a general theme related to the subjects already covered in Part 3.

The cards for Part 3 are on pages C6–C7 of the colour section.

Test 4

READING AND USE OF ENGLISH (1 hour 30 minutes)

Part 1

For questions **1–8**, read the text below and decide which answer (**A**, **B**, **C** or **D**) best fits each gap.

Mark your answers **on the separate answer sheet.**

There is an example at the beginning (**0**).

0	**A**	lingering	**B**	enduring	**C**	unceasing	**D**	perennial

0	A	B	C	D
	▭	▬	▭	▭

The importance of saving plastic

Many artefacts of **(0)** .... cultural significance from the last century were made from plastic. It was always confidently assumed that this rather **(1)** .... material was virtually indestructible. Now that some of these artefacts have become museum **(2)** ...., we have discovered that this **(3)** .... was sadly mistaken.

The degradation of plastics is worrying both scientists and historians, who are racing against time to save our plastic heritage before it **(4)** .... into dust. Our love affair with plastics **(5)** .... in large part from the fact they can be moulded into just about any shape imaginable. When it comes to longevity, however, they have a serious **(6)** ....: their chemical structure breaks down when they are exposed to air and sunlight.

Many now argue that we must consider the cultural **(7)** .... we will be leaving future generations. Without urgent **(8)** .... many artefacts will be lost forever. But developing effective conservation strategies is difficult because what works to preserve one type of plastic can have a catastrophic effect on the lifespan of another.

	A	B	C	D
1	**A** trivial	**B** routine	**C** customary	**D** mundane
2	**A** items	**B** articles	**C** pieces	**D** objects
3	**A** concept	**B** premise	**C** notion	**D** proposition
4	**A** crumbles	**B** shatters	**C** erodes	**D** shrivels
5	**A** starts	**B** sparks	**C** stems	**D** sprouts
6	**A** fault	**B** snag	**C** stigma	**D** flaw
7	**A** bequest	**B** legacy	**C** endowment	**D** heirloom
8	**A** intervention	**B** interception	**C** interference	**D** intercession

Part 2

For questions **9–16**, read the text below and think of the word which best fits each space. Use only one word in each space. There is an example at the beginning (**0**). Write your answers **IN CAPITAL LETTERS on the separate answer sheet.**

Example: | **0** | O | N |

Is nothing impossible?

It is certainly the case that believers in 'nothing is impossible' base their blind optimism **(0)** .... a kernel of truth. Strictly **(9)** ...., as logicians are keen to remind us, only **(10)** .... which involves a logical contradiction is impossible. So two plus two cannot equal five, **(11)** .... can there ever be any truly square circles. However, the limits that most of us have in **(12)** .... when we worry about our lives are rarely logical.

For as **(13)** .... as something remains logically possible, some people can't help **(14)** .... wonder if their dream might become reality. This is exacerbated by the fact that our culture encourages people to **(15)** .... big and believe that 'impossibility' is nothing more than the creation of a negative mind.

It is far simpler, though, to concentrate on levels of difficulty and chances of success. If the former are too high and the latter too low, there's hardly any point in adding 'but it isn't impossible, **(16)** .... enough desire or support'.

Part 3

For questions **17–24**, read the text below. Use the word given in capitals at the end of some of the lines to form a word that fits in the space in the same line. There is an example at the beginning (**0**). Write your answers **IN CAPITAL LETTERS on the separate answer sheet**.

Example: | **0** | U | N | P | R | E | C | E | D | E | N | T | E | D | | | | | | |

Living in a digital age

Today, our life is filled with noise, words and images to an **(0)** .... degree,	**PRECEDE**
with people spending much of their time connected to different forms of	
media. Consider the 'quiet carriage' signs found on many UK trains; these are	
indications that passengers must be **(17)** .... requested to refrain from	**SPECIFY**
talking on their mobile phones.	
The greatest advantages of wired living are easily **(18)** .... Plugged into	**NUMERATE**
the web, we can research and **(19)** .... much of humanity's gathered	**REFER**
knowledge – in minutes. We have almost **(20)** .... capabilities, and we	**IMAGINE**
are becoming increasingly adept at using them. When we are unplugged,	
we can demonstrate the capacity to make decisions and to act on our own	
(21) .... We therefore need to appreciate the value of being able to	**INITIATE**
function both online and offline. However **(22)** .... technology becomes	**PERVADE**
in the future, we need to think **(23)** .... and to learn how to assess its	**CRITIC**
(24) .... as well as its advantages in order to make discerning use of	**COMING**
it in our lives.	

Part 4

For questions **25–30**, complete the second sentence so that it has a similar meaning to the first sentence, using the word given. **Do not change the word given**. You must use between **three** and **eight** words, including the word given. Here is an example (**0**).

Example:

0 Do you mind if I watch you while you paint?

objection

Do you .... you while you paint?

0	have any objection to my watching

Write **only** the missing words **on the separate answer sheet**.

---

25 How likely is it that Tom will get a place in the team?

chances

What .... getting a place in the team?

26 It has never been explained why he decided to relinquish his position as director.

decision

No .... to relinquish his position as director.

27 Sam doesn't think he'll be able to come with us at the weekend.

prospect

Sam sees .... to come with us at the weekend.

28 Harry has worked hard but it remains to be seen whether he'll win the prize.

time

Harry has worked hard but .... whether he'll win the prize.

29 Luigi decided not to bring up the subject of his salary at the first meeting.

no

Luigi decided to .... the subject of his salary at the first meeting.

30 The professor said that, as far as he knows, the results of the research are accurate.

best

The professor said that .... the results of the research are accurate.

Part 5

You are going to read a magazine article about graphic novels. For questions **31–36**, choose the answer (**A**, **B**, **C** or **D**) which you think fits best according to the text. Mark your answers **on the separate answer sheet**.

Graphic novels: a fresh angle on literature

Has the graphic novel – a fictional story presented in comic-strip format – finally become intellectually respectable?

Graphic novels have just landed with an almighty *kersplat*. Ten days ago, two such works were shortlisted for the Shakespeare Book Awards for the first time in the history of the prize, in two different categories. This was no publicity stunt: neither panel knew what the other had done. This is, surely, the moment when the graphic book finally made its entrance into the respectable club room of high literature. Hang on, though: can you compare a graphic novel with the literary kind? Wouldn't that be like comparing a painting with a music video? Or is it time we started seeing them as comparable mediums for storytelling? If so, what next?

Robert Macfarlane, the chairman of another major literary award, says he has no objection in principle to a graphic novel being submitted for the prize. In fact, he has taught one, Art Spiegelman's *Maus*, alongside the works of Russian writer Tolstoy and *Don Quixote* (by the Spanish writer Miguel de Cervantes) at the University of Cambridge, where he works in the English Faculty. 'The idea of outlawing the graphic novel doesn't make any sense to me,' he says. 'I don't segregate it from the novel. The novel is always eating up other languages, media and forms.' Graphic fiction, he says, is 'another version of the novel's long flirtation with the visual'. This is, he declares, 'a golden age for the graphic novel'.

And he's right. We are seeing a boom in graphic novels. Since *Maus* was awarded a Pulitzer Prize in 1992, they have gone on to devour every literary genre going. But so far, graphic novels have politely stood aside and let conventional books win the big prizes. Now they want the vote. Fighting for the graphic novelists' cause, astonishingly, are some hefty prize-winning writers. The English novelist and poet A. S. Byatt is passionately in favour of graphic novels competing with regular ones. Byatt, who is a huge fan of Spiegelman's *Maus*, thinks that French-Iranian artist Marjane Satrapi's graphic novel *Persepolis* stands 'head and shoulders above most novels being produced. It's more interesting and more moving. It's able to be serious because it can carry itself along on this unserious form. It allowed her to be witty about things that are terrible. And that's why it's a major work of art'.

The genius of the graphic novel, as the English writer Philip Pullman explains, is that it can bring into play so many levels of narrative by layering them on top of each other. Take American Alison Bechdel's brilliant *Are You My Mother?* – in a single page, she can depict a memory of being with her mother in her childhood, dialogue between herself and her mother as they chat on the phone in the present, plus an image of herself toiling at her desk, trying to write her memoir. And what Bechdel and her mum are saying on the phone links to the diaries of the early 20th-century writer Virginia Woolf, which Bechdel also brings to visual life. Try doing that with words – it would take a chapter. Bechdel does it in a few panels. That, in the end, is precisely what keeps graphic literature so distinct from prose narrative.

Graphic novels and traditional novels demand, to be sure, the same amounts of time, intellect and artistry from their authors. But that doesn't mean they're the same thing. A few years on, will you be clicking the buy button on a graphic novel as happily as you'd pick up a work by a traditional novelist? Even Bechdel confesses that her reading habits are still struggling out of the past. 'Honestly, I would be slightly more inclined to pick up a non-graphic work,' she says. 'At this point, there's not a huge number of graphic novels that are about topics that interest me. But that, too, is changing. We're becoming more visually literate. There's some reason for these graphic novels creeping into the canon. We're reading differently from how we used to 200 years ago.'

31 What does the writer say about the nomination of two graphic novels for the Shakespeare Book Awards?

A It revealed the closed-mindedness of the literary establishment.
B It was a result of confusion among members of the panel.
C It generated debate about the true purpose of the prize.
D It was not deliberately calculated to attract people's attention.

32 What does Robert Macfarlane suggest about graphic novels?

A Their long-term success has now been assured.
B Their banning from literature courses has backfired.
C They are a logical step in the development of fiction.
D They tend to be less innovative than traditional novels.

33 In the third paragraph, the writer suggests that, in the past, writers of graphic novels

A lacked the support of influential figures.
B were systematically discriminated against.
C tended to accept their inferior social standing.
D underappreciated the importance of literary awards.

34 The writer discusses Alison Bechdel's book to make the point that graphic novels

A can have just as much narrative depth as traditional novels.
B are able to incorporate a surprising range of different voices.
C can represent the workings of memory in sophisticated ways.
D enable writers to deal with different aspects of a story at once.

35 Bechdel is quoted in the last paragraph to make the point that

A interest in graphic novels reflects a more general trend.
B many readers lack the skills to fully appreciate graphic novels.
C it is difficult to persuade people to take graphic novels seriously.
D graphic novels are far outnumbered by quality traditional novels.

36 In this article, the writer is

A analysing the preoccupations of graphic novelists.
B outlining the origins of graphic novels.
C describing the working practices of graphic novelists.
D evaluating the merits of graphic novels.

Part 6

You are going to read an article about London Zoo. Seven paragraphs have been removed from the extract. Choose from the paragraphs **A–H** the one which fits each gap (**37–43**). There is one extra paragraph which you do not need to use. Mark your answers **on the separate answer sheet.**

London Zoo's new Tiger Territory

London Zoo, one of the oldest in the world, is an architectural jumble. Has its £3.6m Tiger Territory put things right?

'We have tried our best to fade into the background,' says Michael Kozdon, architect of the new £3.6m Tiger Territory at London Zoo. It's not often you hear an architect say that, but then it's not often you have a pair of endangered Sumatran tigers called Jae Jae and Melati as clients, either. 'In the past,' continues Kozdon, 'animal enclosures were all about creating an iconic architectural statement. Now the emphasis is on animal welfare, on bringing visitors as close to the creatures as possible. Our aim is to disappear.'

37

The enclosure's sinuous silhouette echoes the pinkish peaks of its neighbour, the Mappin Terraces, a man-made range of rocky mountains that have long poked their summits above the trees, bringing a surreal air to this strange corner of the park. Built in 1914, this elevated landscape was the result of a clause governing the zoo's expansion: an additional land grab of four acres would only be allowed if the animals they housed could be visible from the rest of the park. Sadly, this sheer geological formation, erupting above the neat neoclassical terraces of north west London, has been barren since 1985, when Pipaluk, the last of the polar bears, was finally moved out after 18 years.

38

'Tigers are avid climbers,' explains Robin Fitzgerald, the zoo's project manager. 'They like to observe their terrain from a towering vantage point, so we've given them a habitat that lets them do exactly that – with a view out over Regent's Park.' Describing how the poles and canopy support each other, he adds: 'It's basically circus tent technology.' Neatly complying with the brief to all but vanish into thin air, this means there is no need for the extra steel structures that are so common in the zoo's other mesh enclosures – such as Cedric Price's famous Snowdon Aviary.

39

The former now provides a cosy den for the tigers, complete with heated rocks to soothe their weary muscles, while the latter has become an elevated area for visitors, with panoramic windows looking out across the Indonesian-inspired landscaping of the enclosure. From here, you can watch the tigers happily splashing about in their pool, or scaling the feeding poles to devour chicken wings and steak.

40

Such practical details are a far cry from many of the zoo's more famous structures, most of which were designed to maximise exotic spectacle. Founded in 1828 as the world's first scientific zoological gardens, the site has become burdened by the weight of its own history. From the start, when it was laid out by Decimus Burton, the zoo employed architects of the highest calibre – leaving it with a legacy of protected buildings.

41

Next door to the Tiger Territory are the bulbous flanks of the majestic elephant and rhinoceros pavilion, designed by Hugh Casson in 1965 to evoke a herd of elephants gathered around a watering hole, their huge rumps jostling for position. Topped with triangular roof lights intended to call to mind nodding heads and swinging trunks, the pavilion was commissioned 'to display these animals in the most dramatic way'.

42

The unavoidable strategy of make-do-and-mend renders London Zoo an inevitably dated institution, laden with rigid monuments conceived in another era that it must now either work with or around building design safari as a wildlife one. Victorian kiosks jostle uncomfortably with mock Tudor clocktowers; lichen-encrusted steel spaceframes cantilever out over brutalist concrete terraces.

43

London Zoo is a fascinating piece of living heritage. With its vastly increased area, near-invisible structure, and strategic re-use of what is already there, the Tiger Territory points a promising way forward. 'The challenge is far greater than it used to be,' says Kozdon. 'Before, architecture led the way. Now the best situation would be to have no buildings at all.'

A However, the Tiger Territory had other constraints to grapple with. With a limited area of 36 acres in one of London's most protected settings, the zoo was forced to modify what it had – in this case, a Victorian stork and ostrich house and a 1960s sea lion viewing platform, both of which had been off-limits to visitors for 30 years.

B But this heritage is a mixed blessing. Take the 1934 penguin pool, a sleek and slender double helix of ramping concrete floating above a blue oval pool. Faces tend to fall when visitors find it empty – the bright white surfaces apparently damaged the penguins' eyes, and the concrete was too hard on their feet. It now stands as an unused but still-loved relic of a bygone age.

C This explains its importance as an important breeding centre for tigers. Tiger Territory's two Sumatran tigers are the most genetically important pair of tigers in Europe. With high hopes for breeding resting on the pair, their cubs would be the first to be born at the zoo for more than 15 years.

D A look inside is telling: the space for visitors far exceeds the narrow nooks created for the immense creatures. The vast structure is now home to bearded pigs and pygmy hippos – tubby, low-slung creatures that seem out of place in the building's soaring, top-lit reaches.

E This architectural jumble all comes to a strange climax in the stripped classical facade of the 1920s aquarium, with its arched entranceway and symmetrical windows now squeezed beneath the colossal mock-rocks of what was once Bear Mountain – itself used to house tanks of water for the fish below.

F This explains why, rather than being held in by a roof, the animals have a fine net canopy stretching above their heads – even though its silken threads are made of 3 mm steel cable. The canopy soars above the treetops of Regent's Park like a giant spider's web.

G Thanks to the Tiger Territory, the skyline of the zoo is now newly populated. The new enclosure boasts several mature plane trees, as well as tall wooden feeding poles fitted with pulleys that hoist big chunks of meat aloft. So, before they can sink their three-inch teeth into lunch, the animals will first have to go up them, which suits their predatory nature.

H These design features demonstrate a new emphasis on animal welfare. This extends to the pairing of the animals, which was meticulously planned. But if needed, the pair can be separated, along with any future cubs, into two different parts of the enclosure, connected by a glass door.

Part 7

You are going to read extracts from an introduction to a book about the study of children. For questions **44–53**, choose from the sections (**A–E**). The sections may be chosen more than once. Mark your answers **on the separate answer sheet**.

In which section are the following mentioned?

the need to be aware of bias in interpretation	**44**	
the lack of documentation on certain children	**45**	
the lack of consensus regarding children's capabilities	**46**	
sources of misleading views on children	**47**	
the interdependence of different approaches to studying childhood	**48**	
a concern about the implication of differences in maturity between children	**49**	
a case for recognising exceptions to traditional characteristics	**50**	
valuing children's opinions in current debates	**51**	
how laws have come to define a child	**52**	
the proportion of children in certain societies	**53**	

Understanding childhood

A

Common sense suggests a child is someone who is young, who is smaller, more immature and vulnerable and in many other ways different to human adults. The pioneer anthropologist of childhood Margaret Mead believed children everywhere were 'pygmies among giants, ignorant among the knowledgeable, wordless among the inarticulate'. Half a century later, there is good reason to challenge this universal prescription for young humanity. Children share in common that they are growing, changing and learning, but they differ in innumerable ways in the expression of growth and change, as well as in the circumstances, goals and extent of their learning. They are not universally seen as weak, wordless or ignorant. Childhood is viewed very differently depending on the geographical area under investigation and the period of time under study as well as the standpoint of the person studying it.

B

This book is as much about studying the cultural beliefs, representations and discourses of childhood as about studying children's physical and psychological immaturity, growth and development. Of course, the two are linked. Key questions are raised about children – their needs, competences, responsibilities and rights. Put simply, how far are they seen as innocents who need protection, nurture and training, and how far as social actors who engage with and contribute to their development, and who have a right to be heard? The near universal adoption of the United Nations Convention on the Rights of the Child has come to symbolize a profound and challenging shift in perspective, especially its emphasis on children's participatory rights. This is reflected in the way this book includes perspectives of children and young people on many of the issues being discussed.

C

The United Nations Convention on the Rights of the Child perceives a child to be anyone under the age of eighteen, which is also consistent with much national and international legislation. But what does this vast cross-section of the world's population – in some countries nearly half the population – have in common that justifies a single formal designation? This is not just an issue of diversity between societies. It is also about the varieties of childhood within the broad age span nought to eighteen years. The child of five months is worlds apart from the child of five years, as is the five year old from the fifteen year old. In many ways, a fifteen-year-old 'child' has more in common with a twenty-five-year-old 'adult' than with a five-year-old 'child'.

D

Developmental psychology has provided detailed descriptions of the many stages and transitions that take place within Western childhoods, which are also reflected in everyday distinctions in the English language – for example, between babies, toddlers, school children, teenagers and young people. Distinguishing kinds of childhood by finely divided ages is not universal. In some societies, children's ages have not always been recorded; their status has been determined by their abilities, their social class or caste and their gender, not by their age. Defining childhood as a distinctive life phase is also premised on assumptions about adulthood. There is good reason to challenge the contrast between the dependent, vulnerable, developing child and the autonomous, mature, knowing adult – for example, by acknowledging situations where adults may be vulnerable and children may be resilient.

E

A guiding principle in planning this book has been to acknowledge wherever possible that knowledge, beliefs and understanding about childhood are culturally situated. Much scientific research on childhood, especially in developmental psychology, has been criticized for presenting its conclusions as universal truths, even though the research was based on children and young people growing up in industrialized societies, especially in Europe and North America. In the same way, dominant discourses of childhood innocence have to be understood in the context of Western history and cultural traditions. This issue applies even more strongly in relation to the study of children's rights, where one of the key debates is about how far the United Nations Convention on the Rights of the Child projects a universalized image of the individualized child which fails to take account of competing cultural traditions.

WRITING (1 hour 30 minutes)

Part 1

Read the two texts below.

Write an essay summarising and evaluating the key points from both texts. Use your own words throughout as far as possible, and include your own ideas in your answers.

Write your answer in **240–280** words.

1

Looking back

Memories are undoubtedly precious to all of us. We can get a huge amount of pleasure and reassurance from the simple act of sitting down with relatives or friends and reminiscing about past events, whether they are amusing incidents from our childhood, teenage adventures or turning points in our lives. Given this, it has to be said that we should be suspicious of any tendency in ourselves or others to fall into the trap of constantly comparing the present with the past. Surely it is better to be focused entirely on the here and now?

Remembering how it was

Memories are more than merely a source of delight; on a more profound level they contribute to our sense of identity. All the experiences we have had make us the people we are today, and without our unique set of memories we would be utterly different. It should not be overlooked that memories can also be unreliable and inconsistent. After all, as the police are well aware, two or three witnesses will often remember the same event in ways that flatly contradict one another. Even close relatives such as siblings will usually have strikingly different memories of a shared family holiday.

Write your **essay**.

Part 2

Write an answer to **one** of the questions **2–5** in this part. Write your answer in **280–320** words in an appropriate style.

---

2 An international newspaper has asked for articles from readers on the theme 'Small World'. You decide to write an article. You should briefly describe some of the effects of global developments in communications, such as travel and social networking. You should also evaluate how the consequences of these developments may affect your own country's cultural identity.

Write your **article**.

3 You are the leader of a local youth group. You have been asked to write a report for your local website on social activities available for young people in your area. In your report you should explain how two or three activities available locally help young people to interact socially. You should also assess the importance of social life in the personal development of young people.

Write your **report**.

4 You recently attended a jobs fair organised for students in their final year at university by a number of major international companies. You decide to write a review of the event for your student newspaper. You should briefly describe one or two jobs which attracted you. Your review should also evaluate how well different companies marketed themselves at the jobs fair in order to attract potential employees.

Write your **review**.

5 Write an answer to **one** of the following two questions based on **one** of the titles below. Write **5(a)** or **5(b)** at the beginning of your answer

(a) John Wyndham: *The Day of the Triffids*
In your literature class you have been discussing the ways in which writers portray characters in their novels. Your tutor has asked you to write an essay comparing the characters of Bill and Josella, and assessing how they come to terms with the difficulties they encounter.

Write your **essay**.

(b) L. P. Hartley: *The Go-Between*
A literary journal has published an article on 'novels with the loss of innocence as a central theme'. It has invited readers to send in letters recommending examples of such novels. You decide to recommend *The Go-Between*. You should briefly describe the story and explain why you think the theme of lost innocence is central to the novel.

Write your **letter.**

LISTENING (40 minutes approximately)

Part 1

You will hear three different extracts.

For questions **1–6**, choose the answer (**A**, **B** or **C**) which fits best according to what you hear.

There are two questions for each extract.

Extract One

You hear one of the owners of a tea supplier in the UK talking on the radio about his business.

1 The man mentions a few clicks of a mouse in order to emphasise that

A the company's website has been designed with ease of use in mind.
B the company makes no attempt to conceal its connections.
C the company's critics have not carried out basic research.

2 What is he doing when he speaks?

A stressing the company's lack of reliance on its backers
B describing the backers' attempts to influence the company
C predicting a reduced role for the backers in future

Extract Two

You hear an academic called Carl Miller talking about playing games.

3 Carl makes a comparison between games and systems in order to suggest how games

A help people to cope with the modern world.
B encourage people to be more competitive.
C reduce people's appreciation of true culture.

4 What is Carl doing when he talks about board games?

A justifying his enjoyment of digital media
B suggesting that humans are inherently social
C emphasising the value of their link to the past

Extract Three

You hear a business presenter called Bill Craven talking about human behaviour.

5 What aspect of great leaders and organisations is Bill focusing on?

A the techniques by which they achieve uniformity
B their ability to persuade others to adopt their ideas
C their capacity to attract followers

6 Bill mentions ball point pens in order to illustrate

A the speed with which technology has developed.
B the negative attitude of some people to change.
C the possible existence of a hidden market.

Part 2

You will hear an airline pilot called Rebecca Martin talking on the radio about a typical day in her job.

For questions **7–15**, complete the sentences with a word or short phrase.

Rebecca says that **(7)** .... are a type of bird that can cause serious problems to aircraft.

Unlike other members of the crew, Rebecca is relieved there won't be a **(8)** .... in Athens.

She says that sometimes there is someone with the title of **(9)** .... on board for long haul flights.

The co-pilot bases his decision regarding **(10)** .... requirements on various criteria.

Rebecca says that to become a pilot nowadays, it is essential to have a **(11)** ...., which was not the case when she started.

She uses the phrase a **(12)** .... to describe her early attitude towards travelling.

She thinks pilots must have what she refers to as a **(13)** .... in order to command authority.

Having the opportunity for a **(14)** .... is a perk of the job that Rebecca enjoyed recently for the first time.

Rebecca mentions the problem of having to work what she calls **(15)** ...., which also impacts on colleagues. .

Part 3

You will hear a radio interview with Olivia Glydon and Ron Partridge, who are hyperpolyglots, people who can speak many languages.

For questions **16–20**, choose the answer (**A**, **B**, **C** or **D**) which fits best according to what you hear.

---

16 Olivia and Ron both say that their motivation for learning so many languages is

A the possibility of communicating with people around the world.
B their fascination with language systems.
C their ability to master languages extremely quickly.
D the challenge of achieving native speaker fluency.

17 What did Ron learn about hyperpolyglots when he was researching his book?

A They do not have any special genetic features.
B They usually have a history of multi-lingualism in the family.
C They are part of a relatively recent phenomenon.
D They usually focus on the same group of languages.

18 When discussing reactions to their hyperpolyglotism, Ron agrees with Olivia that

A people often make the wrong assumptions about their personalities.
B it is surprising how much attention they attract.
C people cannot see the point of learning so many languages.
D it is touching how eager people are to help them.

19 How does Olivia feel about spending so much time on the internet?

A proud of the intensity with which she studies
B defensive about the choices she makes
C worried that she is becoming isolated from her friends
D embarrassed about her enjoyment of soap operas and chat shows

20 What point does Ron make about one East Asian language?

A He finds it particularly appropriate in one situation.
B He hopes to keep it alive for posterity.
C It has not kept up with modern developments.
D It has a special religious significance among its speakers.

Part 4

You will hear five short extracts in which people are talking about commuting

TASK ONE

For questions **21–25**, choose from the list **(A–H)** what general concern each speaker has about commuting.

TASK TWO

For questions **26–30**, choose from the list **(A–H)** how each speaker feels now about their journey.

While you listen, you must complete both tasks.

TASK ONE

A the unproductive use of time

B the possible cost to mental health

C the lack of investment in public transport

D the harm to the environment

E the potential risk of injury

F the tiredness it causes

G the difficulty in avoiding car use

H the increasing expense

Speaker 1		**21**
Speaker 2		**22**
Speaker 3		**23**
Speaker 4		**24**
Speaker 5		**25**

TASK TWO

A pleased that it is relatively short

B grateful to have some time for reflection

C frustrated by fellow commuters

D resigned to making the best of it

E aware of the health benefits

F hopeful of a change in routine

G determined not to continue commuting

H appreciative of the surroundings

Speaker 1		**26**
Speaker 2		**27**
Speaker 3		**28**
Speaker 4		**29**
Speaker 5		**30**

SPEAKING (16 minutes)

There are two examiners. One (the interlocutor) conducts the test, providing you with the necessary materials and explaining what you have to do. The other examiner (the assessor) will be introduced to you, but then takes no further part in the interaction.

Part 1 (2 minutes)

The interlocutor first asks you and your partner a few questions which focus on information about yourselves.

Part 2 (4 minutes)

In this part of the test you and your partner are asked to talk together. The interlocutor places a set of pictures on the table in front of you. There may be only one picture in the set or as many as seven pictures. This stimulus provides the basis for a discussion. The interlocutor first asks an introductory question which focuses on two of the pictures (or in the case of a single picture, on aspects of the picture). After about a minute, the interlocutor gives you both a decision-making task based on the same set of pictures.

The pictures for Part 2 are on page C5 of the colour section.

Part 3 (10 minutes)

You are each given the opportunity to talk for two minutes, to comment after your partner has spoken and to take part in a more general discussion.

The interlocutor gives you a card with a question written on it and asks you to talk about it for two minutes. After you have spoken, the interlocutor asks you both another question related to the topic on the card, addressing your partner first. This procedure is repeated, so that your partner receives a card and speaks for two minutes and a follow-up question is asked.

Finally, the interlocutor asks some further questions, which lead to a discussion on a general theme related to the subjects already covered in Part 3.

The cards for Part 3 are on pages C6–C7 of the colour section.

CAMBRIDGE ENGLISH
Language Assessment
Part of the University of Cambridge

Do not write in this box

SAMPLE

Candidate Name
If not already printed, write name in CAPITALS and complete the Candidate No. grid (in pencil).

Centre No.

Candidate Signature

Candidate No.

Examination Title

Examination Details

Centre

Supervisor:
If the candidate is ABSENT or has WITHDRAWN shade here

Candidate Answer Sheet 1

Instructions

Use a PENCIL (B or HB). Rub out any answer you wish to change using an eraser.

Part 1: Mark ONE letter for each question.

For example, if you think **B** is the right answer to the question, mark your answer sheet like this:

0 A B C D

Parts 2, 3 and 4: Write your answer clearly in CAPITAL LETTERS.

For Parts 2 and 3 write one letter in each box. For example:

0 EXAMPLE

Part 1

1	A	B	C	D
2	A	B	C	D
3	A	B	C	D
4	A	B	C	D
5	A	B	C	D
6	A	B	C	D
7	A	B	C	D
8	A	B	C	D

Part 2

Do not write below here

9		9 1 0 u
10		10 1 0 u
11		11 1 0 u
12		12 1 0 u
13		13 1 0 u
14		14 1 0 u
15		15 1 0 u
16		16 1 0 u

Continues over →

CPE R1 DP754/190

Part 3	Do not write below here
17	17 1 0 u
18	18 1 0 u
19	19 1 0 u
20	20 1 0 u
21	21 1 0 u
22	22 1 0 u
23	23 1 0 u
24	24 1 0 u

Part 4	Do not write below here
25	25 2 1 0 u
26	26 2 1 0 u
27	27 2 1 0 u
28	28 2 1 0 u
29	29 2 1 0 u
30	30 2 1 0 u

SAMPLE

denote Print Limited 0121 520 5100

CAMBRIDGE ENGLISH
Language Assessment
Part of the University of Cambridge

Do not write in this box

SAMPLE

Candidate Name
If not already printed, write name in CAPITALS and complete the Candidate No. grid (in pencil).

Candidate Signature

Examination Title

Centre

Centre No.

Candidate No.

Examination Details

0	0	0	0
1	1	1	1
2	2	2	2
3	3	3	3
4	4	4	4
5	5	5	5
6	6	6	6
7	7	7	7
8	8	8	8
9	9	9	9

Supervisor:
If the candidate is ABSENT or has WITHDRAWN shade here

Candidate Answer Sheet 2

Instructions

Use a PENCIL (B or HB). Rub out any answer you wish to change using an eraser.

Parts 5, 6 and 7: Mark ONE letter for each question.

For example, if you think **B** is the right answer to the question, mark your answer sheet like this:

0	A	B	C	D

Part 5

31	A	B	C	D
32	A	B	C	D
33	A	B	C	D
34	A	B	C	D
35	A	B	C	D
36	A	B	C	D

Part 6

37	A	B	C	D	E	F	G	H
38	A	B	C	D	E	F	G	H
39	A	B	C	D	E	F	G	H
40	A	B	C	D	E	F	G	H
41	A	B	C	D	E	F	G	H
42	A	B	C	D	E	F	G	H
43	A	B	C	D	E	F	G	H

Part 7

44	A	B	C	D	E	F
45	A	B	C	D	E	F
46	A	B	C	D	E	F
47	A	B	C	D	E	F
48	A	B	C	D	E	F
49	A	B	C	D	E	F
50	A	B	C	D	E	F
51	A	B	C	D	E	F
52	A	B	C	D	E	F
53	A	B	C	D	E	F

CPE R2 denote Print Limited 0121 520 5100 DP755/191

CAMBRIDGE ENGLISH
Language Assessment
Part of the University of Cambridge

Do not write in this box

SAMPLE

Candidate Name
If not already printed, write name in CAPITALS and complete the Candidate No. grid (in pencil).

Candidate Signature

Examination Title

Centre

Supervisor:
If the candidate is ABSENT or has WITHDRAWN shade here

Centre No.

Candidate No.

Examination Details

0	0	0	0
1	1	1	1
2	2	2	2
3	3	3	3
4	4	4	4
5	5	5	5
6	6	6	6
7	7	7	7
8	8	8	8
9	9	9	9

Test version: A B C D E F J K L M N

Special arrangements: S H

Candidate Answer Sheet

Instructions

Use a PENCIL (B or HB).
Rub out any answer you wish to change using an eraser.

Parts 1, 3 and **4:**
Mark ONE letter for each question.

For example, if you think **B** is the right answer to the question, mark your answer sheet like this:

0	A	B	C

Part 2:
Write your answer clearly in CAPITAL LETTERS.

Write one letter or number in each box.
If the answer has more than one word, leave one box empty between words.

For example:

0	N	U	M	B	E	R		1	2				

Turn this sheet over to start.

CPE L

DP756/192

SAMPLE

Part 1

1	A	B	C
2	A	B	C
3	A	B	C
4	A	B	C
5	A	B	C
6	A	B	C

Part 2 (Remember to write in CAPITAL LETTERS or numbers)

		Do not write below here
7		7 1 0 u
8		8 1 0 u
9		9 1 0 u
10		10 1 0 u
11		11 1 0 u
12		12 1 0 u
13		13 1 0 u
14		14 1 0 u
15		15 1 0 u

Part 3

16	A	B	C	D
17	A	B	C	D
18	A	B	C	D
19	A	B	C	D
20	A	B	C	D

Part 4

21	A	B	C	D	E	F	G	H
22	A	B	C	D	E	F	G	H
23	A	B	C	D	E	F	G	H
24	A	B	C	D	E	F	G	H
25	A	B	C	D	E	F	G	H
26	A	B	C	D	E	F	G	H
27	A	B	C	D	E	F	G	H
28	A	B	C	D	E	F	G	H
29	A	B	C	D	E	F	G	H
30	A	B	C	D	E	F	G	H

denote Print Limited 0121 520 5100

Visual materials for the Speaking test

1A

1B

1C

2A

2B

2C

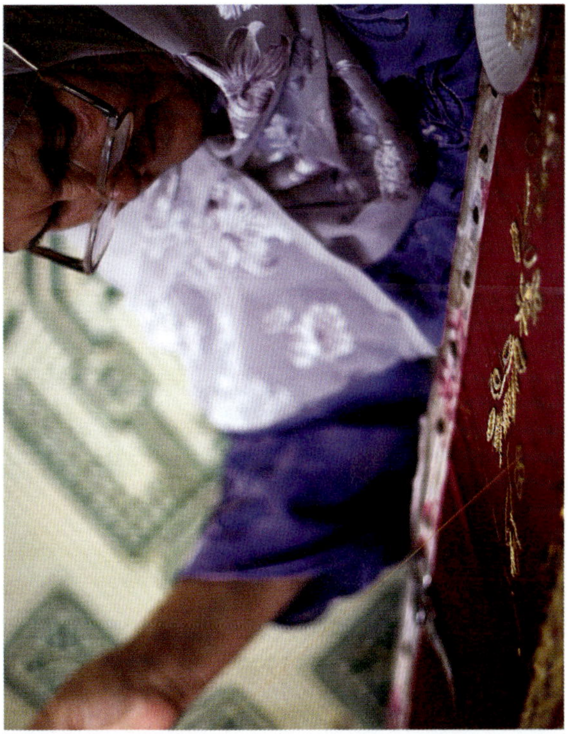

Company planning – New employees

3A

3B

3C

3D

TV documentary series – Lifestyles

4A

4B

TEST 1

Prompt card 1a

What helps people to cooperate with others?

- personalities
- responsibilities
- objectives

TEST 2

Prompt card 2a

How important is it to celebrate the special occasions in our lives?

- traditions
- relationships
- memories

TEST 3

Prompt card 3a

Is it better to plan or to leave things to chance?

- pressure
- security
- opportunity

TEST 4

Prompt card 4a

What are the advantages and disadvantages of parents telling their children what to do?

- safety
- learning
- responsibility

TEST 1

Prompt card 1b

What can be gained by learning in a group?

- different ages
- different skills
- different abilities

TEST 2

Prompt card 2b

How easy is it for young people to learn about important events in history?

- books
- films
- museums

TEST 3

Prompt card 3b

What part does chance play in success?

- sport
- business
- the arts

TEST 4

Prompt card 4b

What are the most important qualities needed to be a successful manager?

- personality
- experience
- communication skills